DISEASES & DISORDERS

Meningitis

Melissa Abramovitz

LUCENT BOOKS
A part of Gale, Cengage Learning

GALE
CENGAGE Learning·

Farmington Hills, Mich • San Francisco • New York • Waterville, Maine
Meriden, Conn • Mason, Ohio • Chicago

GALE
CENGAGE Learning™

LIBRARY OF CONGRESS CATALOGING-IN-PUBLICATION DATA

Abramovitz, Melissa, 1954-
  Meningitis / by Melissa Abramovitz.
    pages cm. -- (Diseases & disorders)
    Includes bibliographical references and index.
    ISBN 978-1-4205-1221-2 (hardback)
    1. Meningitis--Juvenile literature. I. Title.
    RC376.A27 2015
    616.8'2--dc23
                                                2014015151

Lucent Books
27500 Drake Rd.
Farmington Hills, MI 48331

ISBN-13: 978-1-4205-1221-2
ISBN-10: 1-4205-1221-8

Printed in the United States of America
1 2 3 4 5 6 7 19 18 17 16 15

Table of Contents

Foreword   4

Introduction
A Dreaded Disease   6

Chapter One
What Is Meningitis?   11

Chapter Two
What Causes Meningitis?   24

Chapter Three
Meningitis Treatment   40

Chapter Four
Living with Meningitis   54

Chapter Five
Preventing Meningitis   66

Chapter Six
The Future   79

Notes   93
Glossary   99
Organizations to Contact   101
For More Information   104
Index   106
Picture Credits   111
About the Author   112

"The Most Difficult Puzzles Ever Devised"

Charles Best, one of the pioneers in the search for a cure for diabetes, once explained what it is about medical research that intrigued him so. "It's not just the gratification of knowing one is helping people," he confided, "although that probably is a more heroic and selfless motivation. Those feelings may enter in, but truly, what I find best is the feeling of going toe to toe with nature, of trying to solve the most difficult puzzles ever devised. The answers are there somewhere, those keys that will solve the puzzle and make the patient well. But how will those keys be found?"

Since the dawn of civilization, nothing has so puzzled people—and often frightened them, as well—as the onset of illness in a body or mind that had seemed healthy before. A seizure, the inability of a heart to pump, the sudden deterioration of muscle tone in a small child—being unable to reverse such conditions or even to understand why they occur was unspeakably frustrating to healers. Even before there were names for such conditions, even before they were understood at all, each was a reminder of how complex the human body was, and how vulnerable.

While our grappling with understanding diseases has been frustrating at times, it has also provided some of humankind's most heroic accomplishments. Alexander Fleming's accidental discovery in 1928 of a mold that could be turned into penicillin has resulted in the saving of untold millions of lives. The isolation of the enzyme insulin has reversed what was once a death sentence for anyone with diabetes. There have been great strides in combating conditions for which there is not yet a cure, too. Medicines can help AIDS patients live longer, diagnostic tools such as mammography and ultrasounds can help doctors find tumors while they are treatable, and laser surgery techniques have made the most intricate, minute operations routine.

This "toe-to-toe" competition with diseases and disorders is even more remarkable when seen in a historical continuum. An astonishing amount of progress has been made in a very short time. Just two hundred years ago, the existence of germs as a cause of some diseases was unknown. In fact, it was less than 150 years ago that a British surgeon named Joseph Lister had difficulty persuading his fellow doctors that washing their hands before delivering a baby might increase the chances of a healthy delivery (especially if they had just attended to a diseased patient)!

Each book in Lucent's Diseases and Disorders series explores a disease or disorder and the knowledge that has been accumulated (or discarded) by doctors through the years. Each book also examines the tools used for pinpointing a diagnosis, as well as the various means that are used to treat or cure a disease. Finally, new ideas are presented—techniques or medicines that may be on the horizon.

Frustration and disappointment are still part of medicine, for not every disease or condition can be cured or prevented. But the limitations of knowledge are being pushed outward constantly; the "most difficult puzzles ever devised" are finding challengers every day.

A Dreaded Disease

Medical science has made major advances in preventing and treating meningitis (inflammation of the lining of the brain and spinal cord) over the past century. More than 90 percent of the people affected by some form of meningitis before the twentieth century died. Today drugs and other treatments have reduced the death rate for those forms to between 10 and 15 percent. Vaccinations that prevent some types of meningitis have significantly reduced the number of people who get sick from the disease as well. However, even with these advances, meningitis remains a dreaded disease throughout the world.

Both physicians and laypersons dread meningitis for several reasons. The British doctor Phil Hammond explains, "As a doctor, meningitis is the disease that you dread coming across as its symptoms are so hard to spot and it can kill so quickly."[1] Another reason for the widespread dread is that the disease can affect anyone of any age and poses special risks for babies and children. The fact that some of the most dreaded forms of meningitis are contagious also contributes to widespread fears.

Recent meningitis outbreaks in the United States—one in 2012 and one in 2013—highlight the fear the disease inspires. These outbreaks also illustrate how rarely seen sources of meningitis can suddenly emerge and change lives with lightning speed.

The 2012 Outbreak

On September 21, 2012, the federal Centers for Disease Control and Prevention (CDC) began to receive reports from state health departments about patients with meningitis who had received spinal injections of methylprednisolone acetate days or weeks earlier. This medication is used to treat severe back pain. Laboratory tests indicated that most of the meningitis patients were infected with a fungus called *Exserohilum rostratum*. This fungus rarely infects humans.

The CDC quickly traced the medication that caused the outbreak to a compounding pharmacy called the New England Compounding Center (NECC) in Massachusetts. Experts discovered that unopened vials of methylprednisolone acetate at NECC were contaminated with *Exserohilum rostratum*. They also determined that about fourteen thousand patients had been injected with contaminated medication between May and September 2012. The patients were all notified, and

An outbreak of deadly fungal meningitis occurred in 2012; its source was traced to the New England Compounding Center (shown), in Framingham, Massachusetts. The CDC reported that more than 750 patients in twenty states had been sickened by the contaminated injections, and 64 had died.

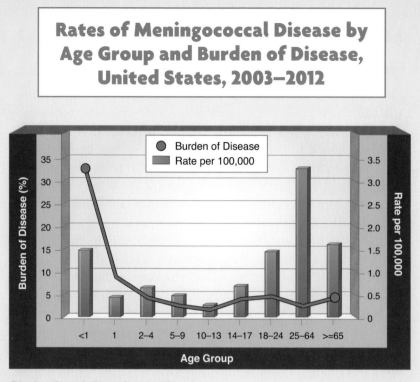

Rates of Meningococcal Disease by Age Group and Burden of Disease, United States, 2003–2012

Taken from: Centers for Disease Control and Prevention.

widespread panic ensued as they rushed to be tested for signs of the brain infection. In December 2012 the CDC reported that more than 750 patients in twenty states had been sickened by the contaminated injections, and 64 had died.

The CDC investigation showed that NECC's failure to sterilize its drug ingredients and areas where the drugs were mixed led to the drug contamination. The investigators are not sure how the fungi originally got into the facility but note that these microorganisms commonly grow in the environment and could have been unknowingly brought in by employees. Had NECC followed proper sterilization procedures, these microorganisms would have been killed. Instead, fungi and several types of bacteria discovered on laboratory surfaces and in the drug ingredients remained in several NECC products.

In October 2012 all products made by NECC were recalled, and the state of Massachusetts shut the company down. Hundreds of patients filed lawsuits, and federal and state prosecutors filed criminal charges against NECC as well. "This was preventable. They failed to properly sterilize this medicine that had to be sterilized,"[2] stated Eric Kastango of the consulting firm Clinical IQ in a *New York Times* article.

Until this outbreak occurred, compounding pharmacies, like other pharmacies, were regulated by state health departments rather than by the stricter rules imposed on most drug manufacturers by the U.S. Food and Drug Administration (FDA). This was because compounding pharmacies were not supposed to manufacture and sell large quantities of medications. Instead, they were originally set up as specialized pharmacies that mixed and sold a small number of injectable medications to doctors' offices and hospitals. They later turned into large-scale drug manufacturing companies whose prices were lower than those of conventional drug manufacturers. State agencies allowed NECC and other compounding pharmacies to operate despite concerns about product quality in years prior to the outbreak.

In November 2013 the U.S. Congress passed the Drug Quality and Security Act to give the FDA authority over compounding pharmacies. Senator Edward Markey, who promoted the law, stated, "This bill will go a long way to ensure that public health is protected and compounded drugs are safe."[3] However, the damage done by NECC cannot be undone. Many survivors of the outbreak have lasting mental and physical disabilities, and many are afraid to receive spinal injections again despite the new law.

The 2013 Outbreaks

Unlike the fungal meningitis outbreak in 2012, the 2013 outbreaks were not caused by peoples' actions. The 2013 outbreaks at several colleges were caused by the sudden appearance of a type of meningococcal bacterium that is not covered by current vaccines in the United States. Meningococcal bacteria are responsible for many of the most serious cases of meningitis. The vaccines given to most college-aged people protect against four types of these bacteria, but not against the type B meningococci that sickened eight students at Princeton University between March and December 2013 and four at the University of California–Santa Barbara in November 2013. Infectious disease experts are not sure why type B meningococci suddenly appeared on American college campuses. These bacteria usually affect infants and are rarely seen in the United States. "This is very unusual. We're all kind of scratching our heads at this point,"[4] William Schaffner of Vanderbilt University told the health news service HealthDay.

Although the number of affected students was relatively small, the outbreaks still triggered widespread fear because meningococcal meningitis is contagious and can have devastating effects. The affected students recovered, but one had to have his feet amputated because of the disease. Campus officials canceled social gatherings and warned students to be cautious about kissing and sharing food and drinks. Preventive antibiotics were given to thousands of students, and the CDC took the extreme step of obtaining emergency supplies of a type B vaccine currently approved for use in Europe but not in the United States. Princeton University paid for vaccinations for all its students.

Many students and their families told the media that the outbreaks generated panic. Jonathan Abboud of the University of California–Santa Barbara told the *Los Angeles Times*, "A lot of students aren't sharing drinks and food as much as they used to. . . . It's on everyone's mind."[5] In the same article Olivia Ravasio stated, "The paranoia is absolutely terrible. Wake up and your neck hurts. On any other day, you think nothing of it, but now it's like, 'Should I go to the hospital? Why does my head hurt?'"[6]

While public health officials do not encourage panic over such outbreaks, they also recognize that informing people about the dangers of meningitis is bound to unleash apprehension. As meningitis expert Andrew W. Artenstein writes in his book *In the Blink of an Eye*, meningitis "has earned its status as one of the most dreaded contagious diseases of nature."[7]

CHAPTER ONE

What Is Meningitis?

The word *meningitis* comes from the Latin word *meninga* and the Greek suffix *itis*. *Meninga* means "membrane," and *itis* means "inflammation." Thus, *meningitis* refers to an inflammation of the membranes (known as meninges) that surround the brain and spinal cord. The French doctor François Herpin first used the term *meningitis* in 1803 to distinguish inflammation of the meninges from inflammation of the brain itself (known as encephalitis). He called the condition "de méningitis ou de méningite"[8] in his book *Meningitis ou Inflammation des Membranes de l'Encephale* (Meningitis or Inflammation of Brain Membranes).

Prior to Herpin's writings, most doctors referred to both meningitis and encephalitis as "brain fever" or "cerebrospinal fever," though the English physician Thomas Willis did refer specifically to inflammation of the meninges when he described an outbreak in 1661. In his description Willis wrote that affected patients showed "a continual raving, or a depravation of the chief faculties of the Brain, arising from an inflammation of the Meninges with a continual fever."[9] Although Willis briefly described meningitis in 1661, it was not until Herpin named the disease in 1803 and the Swiss physician Gaspard Vieusseux published the first detailed clinical report in 1805 that meningitis became widely known.

Once meningitis was known as a distinct disease, doctors reported outbreaks throughout the world. The first reported cases in the United States occurred in 1806, when doctors

Thomas Willis

The British physician Thomas Willis (1621–1675) was the first doctor known to have written about meningitis. Willis was born on January 27, 1621, on his family's farm in Wiltshire, Great Britain. He attended Oxford University and received his medical degree in 1646. He then served as King Charles I's physician and taught natural philosophy at Oxford. He also ran a busy, successful private medical practice.

Willis is widely known for having written several medical textbooks about the brain. He pioneered brain research and is credited with discovering and describing many parts of the human brain. One of his best-known discoveries was the so-called circle of Willis. This circular-shaped cluster of blood vessels sits at the base of the brain. Its structure allows blood to flow equally to both sides of the brain.

Willis also proposed novel theories about the causes of many brain disorders and was one of the first to connect the workings of the brain with the conscious mind. Most doctors in his era and beyond did not associate the brain with thinking or with directing other body parts to function. As an article in *Notes and Records of the Royal Society* states, "He was in advance of his time in supposing that nervous energy, though derived from the bloodstream, has its origin in the brain."

Charles Symonds. "Thomas Willis, F.R.S. (1621–1675)." *Notes and Records of the Royal Society*, July 1960, p. 95.

British physician Thomas Willis was the first physician to write about meningitis.

Lothario Danielson and Elias Mann described an outbreak in Medfield, Massachusetts, in the *Medical and Agricultural Register*. After the 1806 outbreak, doctors reported that the disease had spread throughout the northeastern United States and then to the remainder of the country. At that time more than 90 percent of the affected patients died because of the serious consequences of inflamed meninges.

The Role of the Meninges

The CDC describes the meninges as "a three-layer jacket inside our heads protecting our brain and spinal cord."[10] Collectively, the brain and spinal cord are known as the central nervous system (CNS), which serves as the body's command center. The brain sends messages to the spinal cord, which consists of bundled nerve fibers, and these nerve fibers branch out to transmit signals to the organs and other parts of the body. These nerve branches are called the peripheral nervous system. Peripheral nerves relay movement instructions to muscles and carry sensory information from the eyes, ears, nose, tongue, and skin to the brain.

A functioning CNS is essential for sustaining life. Without it, organs such as the heart cannot perform properly. Human anatomy therefore goes to great lengths to protect this vital system. The brain is encased in the bones that constitute the skull, and the spinal cord is housed in bones called vertebrae. The three layers of meninges that sit under these protective bones provide still another shield from harm.

The outermost layer of the meninges, the dura mater, consists of tough, inflexible tissue. The term *dura mater*, in fact, means "hard mother" in Latin. This layer of the meninges not only protects the CNS, but it also separates the brain into compartments. One section of the dura mater called the falx cerebri separates the brain's two hemispheres, or halves. Another section, the falx cerebelli, separates the four lobes, or main areas, of the cerebral cortex. The brain's cortex mainly directs thinking and reasoning.

The part of the dura mater that surrounds the outside of the brain and spinal cord is separated from the skull and vertebrae by a space called the epidural space. Another space, the subdural space, sits under the dura mater and separates it from the next layer of the meninges—the arachnoid mater, so named because the blood vessels and nerve fibers in this layer give it a spider web–like appearance. The Greek word *arachne* means "spider," and *oid* means "like."

The arachnoid mater is much thinner than the dura mater. Underneath it lies the subarachnoid space that contains cerebrospinal fluid. Cerebrospinal fluid is the clear liquid that helps the meninges cushion and protect the brain. It also brings nutrients and removes waste from brain cells. Cerebrospinal fluid fills the interior spaces in the brain that separate its parts and the central canal inside the spinal cord.

Beneath the subarachnoid space is the thinnest layer of the meninges—the pia mater. The Latin word *pia* means "pious" or "tender." The pia mater contains the choroid plexus structures that produce cerebrospinal fluid. Blood vessels and epithelial cells that line choroid plexuses interact with blood to manufacture this important protective fluid. Besides creating cerebrospinal fluid, choroid plexuses also play a role in the blood-brain barrier. This protective mechanism separates circulating blood from the CNS to prevent most microorganisms and poisons that get into the bloodstream from reaching the brain and spinal cord. The blood-brain barrier does allow smaller molecules such as oxygen, nutrients, and hormones to cross from the bloodstream into the CNS. Tightly packed endothelial cells in blood vessels in the choroid plexuses are mostly responsible for creating the blood-brain barrier. Tightly packed cells in several other areas of the CNS help with this process.

Inflammation of the Meninges

The vital functions performed by the meninges can be disrupted if these membranes become inflamed. Inflammation (swelling) can cause brain cells to die and can weaken the

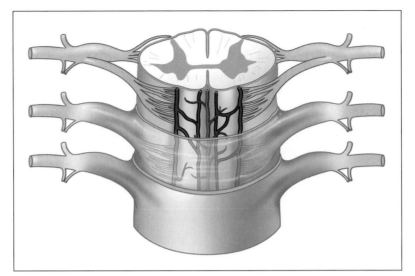

The meninges form a three-layer "jacket" that surrounds and protects the brain and spinal cord.

blood-brain barrier. Since the brain is enclosed in a tight space, inflammation can also increase the pressure in various areas. Increased pressure leads to severe pain, and damaged or dead cells can prevent functions such as thinking, hearing, or brain-controlled processes like breathing from occurring. Other symptoms of meningitis reflect other consequences of inflammation, such as fever, which occurs when the immune system launches an attack to overcome an infection.

Not all patients have identical symptoms or consequences from meningitis, but most do have the fever, severe headache, stiff neck, vomiting, and confusion that doctors have described since meningitis was identified. The 1806 report on the Medfield, Massachusetts, outbreak by Danielson and Mann, for example, revealed that all of the affected people were "suddenly taken with violent pain in the head and stomach succeeded by cold chills and followed by nausea and puking . . . [and] the heat of the skin becomes much increased."[11]

Doctors have identified additional characteristic symptoms and signs of meningitis since these early reports. For instance, a characteristic of the stiff neck seen in meningitis is that the

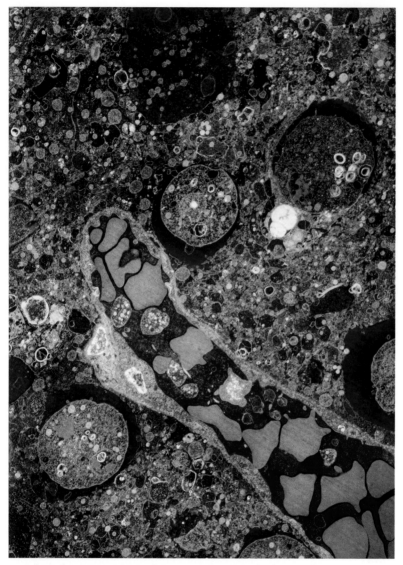

A colored transmission electron micrograph shows the meningitis causing protozoa (yellow) in the meninges.

patient cannot bend the neck downward. This is known as nuchal rigidity. Many patients also show Kernig's sign and Brudzinski's sign. Kernig's sign was first described by the Russian neurologist Vladimir Kernig in 1882. To detect Kernig's sign, a patient lies down and a doctor bends the individual's thigh at the hip. The doctor then tries to extend the patient's knee. This is so painful that the patient's knee cannot straighten all the way in those with a positive Kernig's sign. To detect Brudzinski's sign (first described by the Polish pediatrician Jozef Brudzinski in 1909), a physician holds one hand behind a patient's head and the other hand on the person's chest while the patient is lying down. The doctor then raises the patient's head. In a positive Brudzinski's sign, the patient involuntarily bends his or her knees. Both Kernig's and Brudzinski's signs result from nerve roots in the spinal cord passing through inflamed meninges. Not all people with meningitis display these signs, but their presence does mean that a patient has meningitis because they are not seen in other diseases.

Like Kernig's and Brudzinski's signs, some of the other symptoms of meningitis depend on which parts of the CNS are affected. When inflammation affects meninges connected to nerves that extend to the arms and legs, this can lead to weakness, numbness, or paralysis of the limbs. When the meninges in areas of the brain that control vision or hearing are inflamed, this can result in over- or under-sensitivity to light or sound. When blood vessels inside the meninges are inflamed, this can lead to the development of blood clots in the brain and result in a stroke. Strokes can occur when blood flow to the brain is blocked.

Inflammation of the meninges in the cerebral cortex leads to the confusion and other thinking disruptions experienced by many patients. As an example of these disruptions, a young woman named Zoe McCallum could not follow doctors' instructions to count backward from one hundred when she had meningitis. Her answers to other questions showed a lack of logical thought and sounded like gibberish. She also could not remember how to post messages on Facebook.

Variations in Symptoms

In addition to these differences in symptoms in individual cases, some symptoms tend to vary in people of different ages. For example, infants under six months old and most elderly people do not show a positive Brudzinski's sign. Physicians believe this is because the immature nervous system in newborns does not display the reflexes that underlie this symptom. They think many elderly people do not show Brudzinski's sign because many have arthritis or spinal disk problems that interfere with reflexes.

Affected infants also tend to cry constantly and have little or no appetite. The fontanelle (the soft spot on infants' heads) may also bulge outward due to the inflamed meninges underneath it. Like infants, small children with meningitis tend to be irritable. They also report leg pain and cold arms and legs more often than older children and adults do.

Symptoms can also vary according to which type of meningitis an individual has. Although all types of meningitis generally include severe headache, stiff neck, vomiting, and confusion, these symptoms are more likely to develop gradually over a period of several days when meningitis is caused by a virus or fungus. Cases caused by bacteria tend to develop and progress very suddenly. Those cases that develop gradually are also more likely to be chronic, or long lasting. Doctors define chronic meningitis as lasting more than four weeks. Acute, or sudden, cases are defined as lasting less than four weeks. About 90 percent of cases of meningitis are acute.

People with meningitis caused by meningococcal bacteria can also show a symptom not seen in other types of the disease—purple spots on the skin. This rash heralds a dangerous and usually fatal complication that results from the bacterial infection spreading from the nervous system to the bloodstream. This complication is called meningococcal sepsis, or meningococcemia. *Sepsis* is a general term used to describe blood poisoning.

The purple rash results from blood seeping from inflamed, damaged blood vessels and collecting under the skin. In very serious cases patients may also develop oozing purple and black sores. These sores result from blood vessels collapsing and the subsequent death of tissues throughout the body. Collapsed blood vessels often lead to very low blood pres-

A Difficult Diagnosis

Many times, meningitis is difficult to diagnose because its symptoms mimic flu. Sometimes, though, it is mistaken for psychiatric illnesses. A patient named Keith McIntyre, for example, began having memory lapses and hallucinations after developing a gum infection and horrific back pain. He was hospitalized when he became incoherent and started raving about bugs crawling on him. During his hospital stay, McIntyre frantically kept asserting that people were out to kill him. He became violent when hospital personnel tried to restrain him. A neurologist who examined him thought he had a mental illness such as schizophrenia, but tests performed by a psychiatrist ruled this out.

Doctors had still not figured out what was wrong when McIntyre stopped breathing and they had to insert a breathing tube. The next day his heart stopped. Doctors restarted it, but he was in a coma for three weeks. One of his physicians finally thought to perform a spinal tap, which revealed that he had meningitis. Bacteria from his infected gums had migrated to his brain and spinal cord and caused a massive infection. Although no one expected him to live, he did survive the ordeal.

sure known as septic shock. When this happens, the blood supply to organs and other body parts is cut off, leading to organ failure and gangrene (tissue death). Cells and tissues cannot live without a blood supply that brings them oxygen and nutrients.

One mother whose two-year-old daughter, Jenny, died from meningococcemia describes how the girl looked several hours after falling ill: "She was purple from head to foot, looking like a burn victim. . . . Less than 36 hours after she had first had the temperature, it was clear that her little body was basically destroyed. Someone explained that the colour she was on the outside—this black, burnt-like appearance—was likely to be

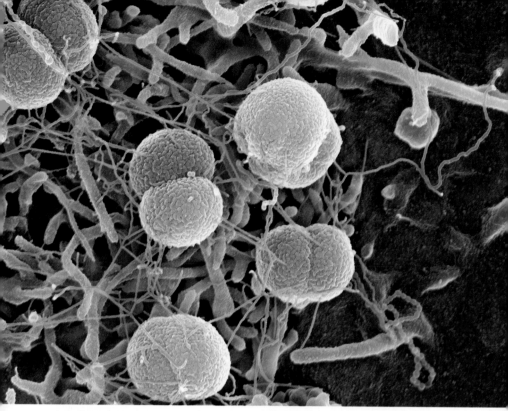

A colored transmission electron micrograph shows meningitis bacteria (orange) that create the disease's symptoms of headache, fever, stiff neck, vomiting, and delirium.

the colour of all her internal organs, her eyes, her brain, every inch of our beautiful daughter."[12]

Diagnosing Meningitis

Symptoms such as a purple rash, fever, and severe headache provide doctors with clues that meningitis is present, but often diagnosing the disease is difficult because similar symptoms exist in other conditions. According to the National Foundation for Infectious Diseases, "Meningococcal disease is often misdiagnosed as something less serious because early symptoms are similar to influenza and other common viral illnesses."[13] Other types of meningitis besides meningococcal meningitis can also mimic flu and can be equally difficult to diagnose. For example, a patient named Kelly had a severe headache, vomiting, and numbness in one side of her face for a month before doctors realized she had viral meningitis. She was in and out of emergency rooms, but doctors kept telling her she had flu, until one finally thought to order tests that revealed meningitis.

In Kelly's case the delayed diagnosis did not lead to horrific results. For many other patients, however, a prompt diagnosis might have saved their lives because it would have led to prompt treatment. Seventeen-year-old Brittany, for example, developed a headache, fever, and vomiting one evening. Her parents took her to a hospital, but doctors thought she had flu and sent her home. When she became unable to feel her legs during the night,

Meningitis Symptoms

Meningtis Symptoms in Adults
These symptoms may not all occur at the same time
Vomiting
Headache
Drowsiness
Seizures
High temperature
Joint aching, joint pain
Stiff neck
Dislike of light
Meningtis Symptoms in Children
These symptoms may not all occur at the same time
A high-pitch moaning cry, whimpering
Dislike of being handled, fretful
Arching back, neck retraction
Blank, staring expression
Difficult to wake up or very lethargic
Fever and may have cold hands and feet
Refusing feeds or vomiting
Pale, blotchy skin color

Taken from: Boston College. University Health Services. "Meningitis." http://www.bc.edu/offices/uhs/education/meningitis.html.

her parents took her back to the hospital. Physicians performed a spinal tap, also known as a lumbar puncture, which is the most important test for diagnosing meningitis. They began treatment, but Brittany soon developed a purple rash and passed away when her organs began shutting down.

A spinal tap involves inserting a hollow needle through the skin of the lower back into the space between two vertebrae. The needle is pushed through the outer layers of the meninges into the subarachnoid space, which contains cerebrospinal fluid. A sample of this fluid is withdrawn and analyzed in a laboratory. The test is extremely painful and can result in a severe headache or other side effects. Thus, it is often difficult for doctors to decide whether a spinal tap is necessary when they suspect that a patient has flu rather than meningitis. As pediatrician William Sears writes, "Because the flu is so common, doctors can't do a spinal tap on every person with simple

A doctor performs a lumbar puncture, or spinal tap, on a patient. Analyzing the cerebrospinal fluid is the most effective way for physicians to accurately diagnose meningitis.

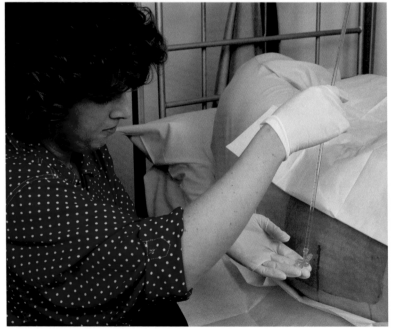

flu symptoms. It is important to examine closely for neck or spinal pain and stiffness."[14] The presence of a stiff neck that is so painful that the patient cannot bend the neck downward is usually enough of an indication of meningitis to spur doctors to perform a spinal tap.

Analyzing the cerebrospinal fluid allows physicians to determine which type of meningitis a patient has. When the fluid appears cloudy instead of clear, this often means the person has bacterial meningitis. Laboratory technicians can determine the type of bacterium by growing cultures in the laboratory or performing a DNA test called polymerase chain reaction to identify which microorganisms are present. Looking at white blood cells (immune system cells) in the cerebrospinal fluid can also help determine the type of meningitis because the human body dispatches different types of white blood cells to fight different types of pathogens. When white cells known as neutrophils predominate, this usually indicates that bacteria are present. An abundance of lymphocytes is a sign that viral meningitis is present, and when eosinophils predominate it usually means a patient has fungal or parasitic meningitis.

In addition to a spinal tap, doctors often perform imaging and blood tests when they suspect meningitis. Imaging tests such as computed tomography (CT) scans or magnetic resonance imaging (MRI) can show swelling in the meninges to confirm a suspected diagnosis. CT scans create computerized three-dimensional X-ray images of internal body parts. MRI imaging uses magnetic coils and radio waves to generate similarly detailed pictures of internal structures.

Doctors also order typical blood tests like the C-reactive protein test and a complete blood count. These tests give an indication of whether inflammation and infection are present, but they cannot identify the type of meningitis present. Used in conjunction with a spinal tap, these blood tests can allow a definitive diagnosis to be made so appropriate treatment can be started. Knowledge about whether a patient has meningitis and identification of the specific cause are both essential in this process.

CHAPTER TWO

What Causes Meningitis?

The five main types of meningitis—bacterial, viral, fungal, parasitic, and noninfectious—each have different causes. The first four types are caused by microorganisms. Scientists did not know that microorganisms existed until the invention of the microscope in 1595 allowed them to view these tiny creatures. Later work by the French chemist Louis Pasteur and the German physician Robert Koch in the late 1800s proved that certain microorganisms cause specific diseases. Prior to these events most people believed that evil spirits or divine punishment were responsible for causing disease.

Meningococcal Meningitis

The first microorganisms that scientists identified as a cause of meningitis were meningococcal bacteria. Other types of bacteria can also cause the disease, but meningococci are responsible for meningitis epidemics. In 1887 the Austrian physician Anton Weichselbaum was the first to isolate and study meningococci, which he found in pus taken from the brains of people who had died from epidemic meningitis. He injected the bacteria into laboratory animals to prove that the bacteria caused meningitis. This resulted in sores and inflammation in the animals' brains. Weichselbaum called the bacteria *Diplo-*

coccus intracellularis meningitidis, but the scientific name was later changed to *Neisseria meningitidis*.

Scientists have discovered numerous subtypes, or serogroups, of meningococci. A serogroup is a group of cells that share common substances on the surface. According to the CDC, "Meningococci are classified into serogroups on the basis of the composition of the capsular polysaccharide. The 5 major meningococcal serogroups associated with disease are A, B, C, Y, and W-135."[15] A capsular polysaccharide is a sugarlike covering found on disease-causing bacteria. The human

French chemist Louis Pasteur proved certain microorganisms cause certain diseases.

immune system identifies and launches an attack on bacteria based on the qualities of this covering.

All types of meningococci enter the body through the nose or mouth. This usually happens after an infected person sneezes or coughs in an enclosed area. This is why meningococcal meningitis often affects people living in close quarters, as in crowded households, college dormitories, and military barracks. The bacteria are also spread to others through kissing or sharing eating utensils.

Once inside the nose or mouth, meningococci attach themselves to cells in the back of the throat using an antenna-like projection called a pilus. They then multiply in the upper airways. Some peoples' immune systems quickly clear out the bacteria, and the individuals do not get sick. But in others the microorganisms continue to multiply, spread to the bloodstream, and cross the blood-brain barrier to infect the meninges. Doctors believe meningococci may be able to breach the blood-brain barrier because they release a poison called endotoxin once they enter the bloodstream. Unlike most poisons, which kill or alter human cells, endotoxin provokes a massive immune response. The assault of immune cells and immune chemicals leads to inflammation that scientists believe weakens the blood-brain barrier.

Although meningococci provoke an immune response, it is very difficult for the immune system to eradicate them once they get into the bloodstream and meninges because they play a trick. A 2009 study at the University of Oxford and Imperial College London revealed that *Neisseria meningitidis* "coats itself with a human protein so that immune cells no longer recognize it as an intruder."[16] The bacteria are then free to continue their assault.

Risk Factors for Illness

Some meningococcal strains, or serotypes, are more likely to evade the immune system than others, and this is one reason that not everyone exposed to the bacteria develops meningococcal disease. Strains with a polysaccharide covering, such

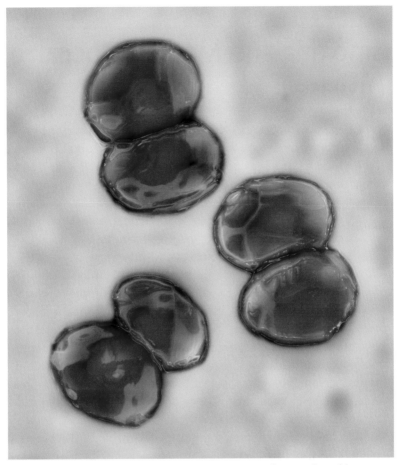

Neisseria meningitidis bacteria (shown) were first isolated by Austrian physician Anton Weichselbaum in 1887.

as A, B, C, W-135, and Y, are much more likely to trick the immune system and cause disease than other strains. Personal qualities of individuals who take in the bacteria also influence whether or not sickness occurs. Although anyone of any age can get sick, babies, children, adolescents, and the elderly are at greater risk than most adults are. People with chronic diseases such as diabetes or heart disease and those with impaired immune systems are also at increased risk of becoming ill.

Personal habits and environmental features also affect disease risk. Smoking, exposure to secondhand smoke, and living

Smoking and Meningococcal Disease

Smoking and exposure to secondhand smoke are among the factors that increase the risk of contracting meningococcal disease. This happens in part because smoke damages cells in the nose and throat and prevents immune cells called monocytes and macrophages from functioning normally. It also happens because smokers are sick more often than other people and tend to carry large numbers of contagious organisms in their breathing passages. Thus, exposure to smoke itself and to smokers both play a role in raising the risk of meningococcal disease for nonsmokers. However, the age of the exposed individuals influences the effects of smoke versus smokers. For young children, exposure to both smoke and smokers raises the risk of developing meningococcal disease. In contrast, a team of British researchers found that close contact with infected smokers, rather than exposure to smoke itself, is usually responsible for the increased risk of meningococcal disease in adolescents. The researchers believe this discrepancy between young children and teenagers occurs because the only smokers young children are likely to have close contact with are family members. Teenagers, on the other hand, are likely to be around many more smokers who harbor meningococci at parties and other social events.

Studies have shown that smoking and exposure to secondhand smoke increase the risk of contracting meningococcal disease.

in dry climates where windblown soil irritates the nose and throat significantly raise the risk of getting meningitis. In fact, meningitis experts believe that the frequent meningococcal epidemics that occur in the so-called meningitis belt in Africa are partly triggered by dry conditions. These epidemics tend to begin during the yearly dry season and taper off during the rainy season. The meningitis belt stretches from Senegal to Ethiopia. It has the highest rate of meningococcal meningitis in the world, with about 100 to 800 cases per 100,000 people per year. Worldwide, there are about 1.2 million cases per year.

Even though some individuals have an increased risk of developing meningococcal disease, it can strike anyone. According to the National Meningitis Association, "The bacteria that cause meningococcal disease reside in the throats and nasal passages of approximately 10 percent of the general population. Researchers are unsure why the bacteria cause some people to become sick while most of the population is not affected."[17]

Other Bacterial Causes

Meningococcus bacteria cause the majority of bacterial meningitis cases worldwide, but in the United States other bacteria cause about 2,900 of the 4,100 cases that occur yearly. The other bacteria generally cause sporadic (individual) cases rather than epidemics that spread from person to person. However, most of these bacteria can also spread from one person to another the same way that meningococci spread.

The most common cause of bacterial meningitis in the United States is *Streptococcus pneumoniae*, also known as pneumococcus. This bacterium also causes pneumonia and ear and sinus infections. It can spread from these sites to the meninges as well as from an infected patient to others through saliva or nasal fluids. A patient named Carolyn, for example, had a serious ear infection. Her eardrum burst, and the infection spread to her meninges. Once there the pneumococci caused the same symptoms that meningococci cause, with the exception of sepsis.

Another bacterium that causes meningitis is *Haemophilus influenzae* type B (Hib). Despite the name, Hib bacteria do not cause influenza. They do cause pneumonia and meningitis and were once the most prevalent cause of bacterial meningitis in children in the United States. However, since most babies in the United States now receive Hib vaccine, Hib causes very few cases of bacterial meningitis in this country. It is still responsible for many cases in places that do not administer this vaccine.

A still-common cause of bacterial meningitis in the United States is *Listeria monocytogenes*. Listeria is spread through contaminated foods. It is often found in soft cheeses made with unpasteurized milk and in luncheon meats. It does not make most people sick when ingested but can be harmful to individuals with impaired immune systems and to pregnant women and babies. An infected pregnant woman can die or pass the infection to her fetus, resulting in miscarriage or premature birth. Listeria meningitis in people with impaired immune systems can also be especially serious. A patient named Jeff, for example, was taking immunosuppressive drugs (drugs that dampen the immune system) to control a disease called ulcerative colitis. This disease results from the immune system attacking cells in the colon (large intestine), causing ulcers. When Jeff ingested food contaminated with Listeria, the ulcers became infected and the bacteria passed into his bloodstream. From there, the bacteria breached his central nervous system (CNS) and caused meningitis.

Viral Meningitis

Although bacteria cause most of the serious and fatal cases of meningitis, cases caused by viruses can also make people very ill and can lead to permanent disabilities. Viral meningitis is more common than bacterial meningitis in the United States— the CDC estimates that 10.9 people per 100,000 contract viral meningitis each year, compared with 3 people per 100,000 for bacterial meningitis.

Doctors refer to meningitis caused by factors other than bacteria as aseptic meningitis. Viral meningitis is the most

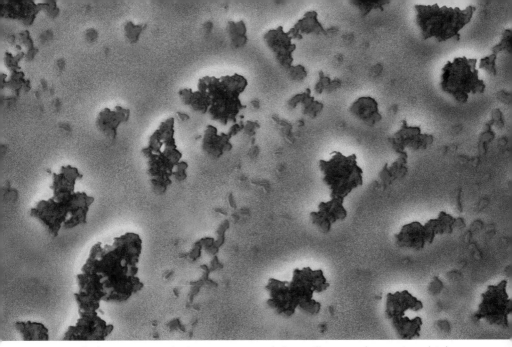

A light micrograph shows *Haemophilus influenzae* bacteria, which were once the prevalent cause of bacterial meningitis in children in the United States.

common form of aseptic meningitis, and enteroviruses are the most common viruses responsible for viral meningitis. Enteroviruses are usually spread through feces. People often become infected after changing a diaper or using the toilet and not washing their hands with soap. Enteroviruses can also be spread through saliva or nasal secretions.

Although some people develop enteroviral meningitis after exposure to others with the disease, most cases of this type of meningitis stem from an internal viral infection that spreads to the meninges. As the CDC explains, "People who are around someone with viral meningitis have a chance of becoming infected with the virus that made the person sick, but they are not likely to develop meningitis as a complication of the illness."[18] This applies to meningitis caused by other viruses such as herpes simplex, varicella zoster (the cause of chicken pox), mumps, HIV (the cause of AIDS), and West Nile virus as well.

Once the meninges are infected, symptoms of viral meningitis are generally identical to those of most types of bacterial meningitis. However, several types of viral meningitis cause unique patterns of symptoms. One form, known as Mollaret meningitis or benign recurrent lymphocytic meningitis, is caused by the herpes simplex viruses that cause cold sores or genital herpes sores. The French neurologist Pierre Mollaret first described Mollaret meningitis in 1944. This type of meningitis tends to go away and then reappear. The length of symptom-free periods varies widely among individuals. Some patients are symptom free for several weeks, while others go for years before experiencing a recurrence. Experts do not know why this illness recurs or why different patterns occur in different patients.

The pattern of symptoms also differs in meningitis caused by lymphocytic choriomeningitis virus (LCMV). Patients with LCMV show symptoms in two phases. The first phase occurs eight to thirteen days after exposure to the virus. Symptoms include fever, headache, muscle aches, nausea, vomiting, and sometimes a sore throat, cough, and chest pain. The patient may then appear to recover, but several days later he or she develops the more specific meningitis symptoms of severe

This rash was caused by viral meningitis, the most common form of aseptic, or non-bacteria-caused, meningitis.

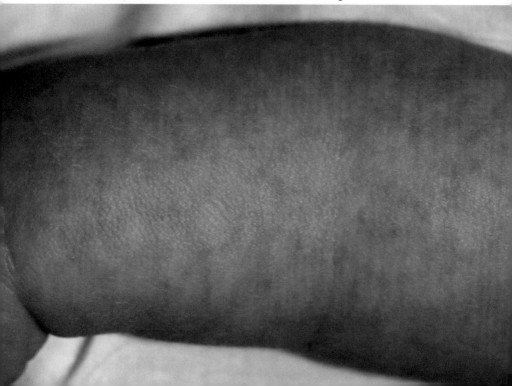

headache, fever, and stiff neck. This phase can last for several days to weeks or even longer.

LCMV is rarely spread from human to human, except in cases of pregnant women passing the virus to the fetus or organ transplant recipients receiving an infected organ. Most of the time people acquire LCMV from mice. The CDC estimates that 5 percent of the wild house mice in the United States carry LCMV in their saliva, urine, and feces. Pet mice and other pet rodents can also carry the virus. Unlike people, rodents do not get sick from LCMV.

People can become infected when exposed to mouse urine, feces, saliva, or nesting materials. Particles containing the virus can be breathed in or enter the body in contaminated food. The virus can also be directly introduced when a mouse bites a person. Public health officials do not know how many people are affected by LCMV, but they do know that the disease is most prevalent in developing countries and in areas where rodents are commonly found in human dwellings.

Parasitic Meningitis

Like LCMV-related meningitis, most cases of parasitic meningitis occur in developing countries. However, the most common form of parasitic meningitis, known as angiostrongyliasis because it is caused by *Angiostrongylus cantonensis* roundworms (rat lungworms), is quickly spreading to places outside these regions. An article in the *Hawai'i Journal of Medicine & Public Health* explains, "The parasite is spreading rapidly around the world, resulting in cases of angiostrongyliasis in places where it had not previously been recorded, facilitated by ease of global travel, globalization of commerce, and climate change."[19]

Rat lungworms start out living in rat lungs. Snails, slugs, freshwater shrimp, crabs, and frogs can become infected when they eat rat feces, and people become infected by eating raw or undercooked snails, frogs, shrimp, or crab. Eating raw snails and other seafood is especially popular in areas of Asia. People can also become infected by eating raw vegetables that were contaminated by infected snails or slugs.

Humans cannot spread the infection to others, but they can become extremely ill or die from angiostrongyliasis, which is also known as eosinophilic meningitis because the human immune system launches immune cells called eosinophils to fight these parasites. Fortunately, many people recover because the parasite cannot live more than a week or so inside humans.

Another parasite that causes meningitis is the single-celled amoeba *Naegleria fowleri*. This parasite enters the human body through the nose when people swim in warm, amoeba-infested lakes, rivers, hot springs, or unchlorinated swimming pools. The parasite can also grow in untreated tap water or in water heaters. In rare instances it enters the body when people irrigate their nasal passages with tap water to relieve sinus pressure. The parasite travels from the nose to the brain, where it multiplies and destroys and eats brain cells. For this reason, *Naegleria fowleri* is sometimes called the brain-eating amoeba.

Besides killing brain cells, *Naegleria fowleri* also causes inflammation both in the meninges and in the rest of the brain. For this reason, the disease that results is called primary amoebic meningoencephalitis. The inflammation and brain cell death that characterize this disease rapidly shut down essential body functions, and death usually occurs in one to twelve days. While primary amoebic meningoencephalitis is uncommon in the United States, it is usually fatal when it strikes. From 2001 to 2010 the CDC reported thirty-two cases. Only three of these patients survived. One survivor was a twelve-year-old girl named Kali Hardig, who became infected while swimming in a lake in Arkansas in July 2013.

Fungal Meningitis

Like parasitic meningitis, fungal meningitis is not contagious. It generally occurs after people inhale fungal spores (single seed-like cells that fungi produce to spread themselves) when the soil where these fungi are found is stirred up by wind or other disturbances. These spores can migrate from the lungs to the CNS to cause meningitis. Rarely, meningitis occurs after

Microorganisms That Cause Meningitis

A variety of microscopic and submicroscopic organisms can cause infectious meningitis.

Viruses are submicroscopic organisms composed of genetic material surrounded by a protein coat. They range from 5 to 300 nanometers in length (one nanometer is one-billionth of a meter). Viruses cannot live or replicate without infecting living cells. Once inside a cell, they hijack the cell's machinery to help themselves reproduce.

Bacteria are single-celled microorganisms that are several micrometers long (one micrometer is one-millionth of a meter). Some can multiply outside a host animal, while others cannot. Bacteria can be harmless, beneficial, or disease causing. Most are shaped like spheres (cocci) or rods (bacilli).

Fungi are neither plants nor animals. They include yeasts and molds and can range from single-celled to multi-celled organisms. Fungal cells are more complex than those of bacteria and viruses— they contain a nucleus and other structures that direct the cells' activities. Not all fungi are harmful, but many can cause serious human diseases.

Like fungal cells, parasitic cells contain a nucleus and other structures. Parasites live on or inside a host animal. Some can reproduce outside the host, but most cannot. All parasites damage their host in some way. They range in size from single-celled amoebas to visible worms.

fungi are introduced directly into the nervous system, as happened during the 2012 outbreak of fungal meningitis in the United States.

Cryptococcus neoformans fungi are responsible for most cases of fungal meningitis. This fungus is found worldwide in soil, particularly in soil contaminated with bird droppings. As with most types of fungal meningitis, cases caused by crypto-coccus generally affect people with impaired immune systems. According to the CDC:

> Because *Cryptococcus* is common in the environment, most people probably breathe in small amounts of the microscopic airborne spores every day. . . . In healthy people, the fungus does not usually cause serious illness because the immune system can fight off the infection. However, in people with weakened immune systems, such as people with HIV/AIDS, the fungus can stay hidden in the body and later reactivate, spreading to other parts of the body and causing serious disease.[20]

Cryptococcal meningitis is in fact a common cause of death in AIDS patients. In Africa, where AIDS is most prevalent, cryptococcal meningitis is responsible for 20 to 25 percent of all AIDS deaths.

A CDC lab technician reviews tests of patients with suspected fungal meningitis after the outbreak from the New England Compounding Center in October 2012.

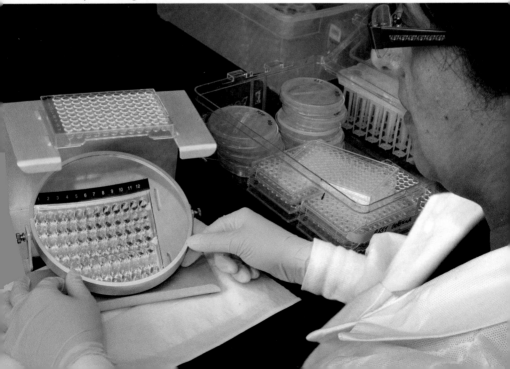

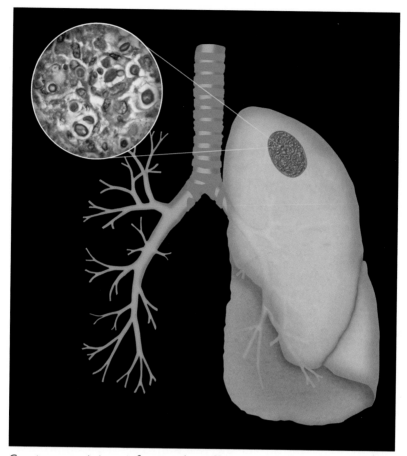

Cryptococcosis is an infection that affects people with HIV/AIDS and other immunodeficient conditions. Infection may cause meningitis or granular growths in the lungs (shown).

Although cryptococcal meningitis occurs throughout the world, some forms of fungal meningitis are restricted to certain areas. For instance, soil in hot, dry places in the southwestern United States is most likely to contain *Coccidioides immitis* or *Coccidioides posadasii* fungi. These fungi cause valley fever when inhaled. There are about 150,000 cases of valley fever each year in the United States, with the numbers rising each year for unknown reasons. In most cases the fungi stay in patients' lungs and cause flu-like symptoms that clear up within a few weeks. About 1 percent of the time, though, the organisms migrate to other body parts, including the meninges. This is most likely to occur in people with weakened immune systems or in those who inhale large numbers of spores. Such cases are likely to be fatal. Without treatment, nearly 100 percent of individuals with coccidioidal meningitis die. With treatment, 20 to 40 percent succumb to the disease.

Noninfectious Meningitis

While most cases of meningitis are caused by fungi, parasites, bacteria, or viruses, the disease can also be caused by drug reactions, head injuries, cancer, or other diseases. Drug-induced meningitis is rare, but the most common medications that trigger this form of the disease are nonsteroidal anti-inflammatory drugs such as ibuprofen; antibiotics; monoclonal antibodies (drugs used to target parts of the immune system); and vaccines such as mumps and hepatitis B vaccines. Anyone can develop meningitis if these drugs inflame the meninges, but people with autoimmune disorders such as lupus are at highest risk. Autoimmune disorders result from the immune system attacking the body's own cells.

Drug-induced meningitis sometimes occurs when drugs injected directly into the nervous system irritate the meninges. Other times drugs taken in pill or injection form cause meningitis by triggering an allergic reaction. This reaction prompts the release of immune cells and chemicals such as cytokines that for unknown reasons settle in and inflame the meninges.

Symptoms of drug-induced meningitis can begin within minutes to hours after the drug is ingested. These symptoms generally go away after the drug is discontinued. However, if the patient ever takes the drug again, the reaction is usually faster and more serious.

Sometimes other diseases or injuries, rather than drugs, are responsible for causing noninfectious meningitis. Diseases such as sarcoidosis and Behcet's disease that cause widespread inflammation can lead to meningitis, and some head injuries that result in brain swelling can do this as well. The most common cause of disease-related meningitis is cancer cells that spread to the meninges. These cancer cells gain entry to the nervous system by producing enzymes such as heparinase that break down the blood-brain barrier. They then settle in the meninges and cause meningitis.

Meningitis caused by cancer cells is known as neoplastic, malignant, or leptomeningeal carcinomatosis meningitis. It can come from any type of cancer but most commonly results from breast, lung, or melanoma cancers. Malignant meningitis is diagnosed in 5 to 25 percent of late-stage cancer patients. Many more cases are undiagnosed and are revealed at autopsy. Overall, 24 to 34 percent of all cancer patients die from malignant meningitis, and an additional 22 to 25 percent die from the combined effects of meningitis and cancer cells. Most patients with this form of meningitis die within four to sixteen weeks, with or without treatment.

Although treatment does not have much of an effect on survival in people with malignant meningitis, it does play a much greater role in some of the other noninfectious and infectious types of meningitis, particularly in bacterial meningitis. This is why doctors emphasize that prompt, appropriate treatment is essential.

CHAPTER THREE

Meningitis Treatment

Prior to the 1900s treatment for meningitis attempted to alleviate symptoms such as pain and fever. Doctors administered plant-based substances such as opium, brandy, and Peruvian bark, but these substances did not alter the course of the disease. As scientists in the late 1800s and early 1900s gained an understanding of the causes of meningitis, effective treatments that saved lives followed.

Antiserum Therapy

The first effective treatments were directed at meningococcal bacteria. In 1904 there was a meningitis outbreak in New York City. About four thousand people became ill, and more than three hundred died. The health department of New York City commissioned the Rockefeller Institute research center to investigate the outbreak and develop a treatment. Simon Flexner, director of the institute, identified the cause as meningococcal bacteria and began experiments to find a treatment. Flexner injected goats and horses with high doses of meningococci to stimulate their immune systems to create antibodies. Antibodies are immune system chemicals that neutralize specific antigens (foreign proteins or organisms). After the animals created antibodies, Flexner took blood samples and separated the blood cells from the blood serum (the liquid part of blood). He found that injecting this serum—known as antiserum because it contains antibodies—into laboratory animals infected with meningococci stopped meningococcal disease from progressing.

Flexner was immunizing the goats and horses—exposing them to a microorganism to provoke an immune response. Once he determined that antibodies produced by one animal could be effectively used by a sick animal, Flexner and his associates began immunizing many horses with meningococci and harvesting blood samples to make large quantities of antiserum. Horses were the animal of choice for this process

In 1904 Dr. Simon Flexner (shown), director of the Rockefeller Institute, identified the cause of a meningococcal meningitis outbreak and began experiments with animals to find a treatment.

Previous Antiserum Treatments

Simon Flexner was the first to develop and use an antiserum to treat meningitis, but he did not invent the procedure. He based his experiments on work done by Emil von Behring and Shibasaburo Kitasato at the Institute of Infectious Diseases in Berlin, Germany, in the 1890s. Behring and Kitasato proved that they could prevent sick animals from dying from diphtheria and tetanus bacteria by injecting them with antiserum from immunized animals. They also demonstrated that injecting uninfected animals with antiserum from immunized animals made the uninfected animals resistant to illness if they were later exposed to the pathogens. Physicians in Europe and the United States were already using a sheep-derived diphtheria antiserum developed by Behring and Kitasato when Flexner decided to try the same technique with meningococcal bacteria.

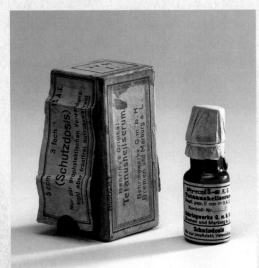

Emil von Behring developed a tetanus antiserum (shown) in 1890 with Japanese scientist Shibasaburo Kitasato.

because their large size means they contain more blood, and large quantities of blood can be extracted without harming them.

Soon afterward, doctors in Ohio had an opportunity to test Flexner's horse antiserum on more than thirteen hundred humans during several meningococcal meningitis outbreaks. Ninety percent of the patients survived when horse antiserum was administered intrathecally (into the spinal cord) within seventy-two hours after the infection occurred. Seventy-five percent of those who received antiserum more than seventy-two hours after infection survived. Flexner concluded that "the earlier the serum injections are begun the better the results."[21]

News of the success of the antiserum led doctors throughout the world to start using it. It became standard meningococcal meningitis treatment until the 1930s, when scientists found that certain dyes made from coal tar could kill bacteria, especially when added to other chemicals. Coal tar is the substance that remains after coal is burned for fuel. One compound called azo, which contains a coal tar dye and the chemical sulfonamide, proved to be especially effective against disease-causing bacteria. Drugs made from sulfonamide (sulfa drugs) soon became the first widely used antibacterials, or antibiotics. The effectiveness and ease of manufacturing these medications quickly led laboratories and doctors to favor them over antiserum treatments, which required the tedious and time-consuming process of immunizing horses and processing their blood serum. Thus, according to the book *In the Blink of an Eye*, "the impact of the new antibacterial drugs was so profound as to render serum therapy almost obsolete overnight."[22]

Antibiotic Treatments

Once sulfa drugs became available, the death rate from bacterial meningitis dropped even more than it had with antiserum. Only about 10 percent of infected people now died. Administering these drugs to people exposed to meningococcal meningitis also prevented symptoms from developing. Sulfa drugs work by preventing bacteria from manufacturing a vitamin called folic acid. They do this by blocking an enzyme called dihydropteroate synthase, which is needed to make the folic acid. Bacteria cannot grow without folic acid, so they soon die. Sulfa drugs do not harm human and other mammal cells because these cells do not manufacture folic acid. They do need this vitamin, but they obtain it when folic acid from an individual's diet crosses from the bloodstream into cell membranes. Unlike human cells, bacterial cell walls do not allow folic acid around them to cross over.

In the 1940s another groundbreaking antibiotic, penicillin, also became available. The British biologist Alexander Fleming discovered penicillin in 1928, but it took some time for scientists to figure out how to produce useful forms of the drug. Unlike sulfa drugs, penicillin and its derivatives work by preventing bacteria from assembling a molecule called peptidoglycan. This molecule is needed to keep bacterial cell walls intact. Without peptidoglycan, the cell walls are extremely weak, and the cells burst. Human cells do not make or need peptidoglycan, so penicillin does not harm human cells.

The discovery of many other new antibiotics that work in different ways to kill bacteria followed the discovery of penicillin. This led many health experts to believe that the infectious diseases that had killed millions of people over the centuries would no longer be a threat. Few people, however, realized that bacteria quickly develop resistance to drugs that kill them. Fleming himself warned the world about this possibility after he discovered penicillin and again during his Nobel Lecture, when he received the Nobel Prize in Physiology or Medicine in 1945. He stated, "It is not difficult to make microbes resistant to penicillin in the laboratory by exposing them to concentrations not sufficient to kill them, and the same thing has occasionally happened in the body."[23]

Resistance occurs because bacteria, like other living creatures, mutate, or change their genetic structure, to increase their chances of survival. Strains that mutate to become resistant to medications replace weaker strains that do not

The Discovery of Penicillin

The Scottish biologist Alexander Fleming accidently discovered penicillin in 1928. He returned to his laboratory at St. Mary's Hospital in London after a vacation and found that a culture of staphylococcus bacteria had become contaminated with a mold. Mold is a type of fungus. Fleming noticed that areas right around the mold were free of bacteria. He grew the mold in cultures and isolated a substance it produces that kills many disease-causing bacteria, including meningococci. He named the substance penicillin, since the mold family that produces it is called penicillium.

At first Fleming did not think penicillin would be useful in medicine because it proved to be difficult to grow in a laboratory. It also seemed to act slowly on bacteria. But other scientists figured out how to mass-produce penicillin in a form that effectively kills many bacteria. It was first used widely in the 1940s. The U.S. Department of Agriculture website states, "Large-scale production of penicillin during the 1940s opened the era of antibiotics and is recognized as one of the great advances in civilization."

U.S. Department of Agriculture. "Penicillin: Opening the Era of Antibiotics." www.ars.usda.gov/Main/docs.htm?docid=12764.

Alexander Fleming developed the antibiotic penicillin from molds, for which he won the Nobel Prize in Physiology or Medicine in 1945.

mutate. Scientists call this phenomenon survival of the fittest. Bacteria began developing resistance to sulfa, penicillin, and other new antibiotics less than one year after their use became widespread.

Some bacteria are more adept at developing resistance than others. Meningococci are extremely proficient at this feat. The CDC explains, "These bacteria have built-in abilities to find new ways to be resistant and can pass along genetic materials that allow other bacteria to become drug-resistant as well."[24] By the 1960s meningococcal bacteria were resistant to most sulfa and penicillin-based drugs. Once again doctors began looking for new ways to control this pathogen.

Bacterial Meningitis Treatment Today

Today there are a variety of antibiotics that are effective against meningococci and other bacteria that cause bacterial meningitis. Cefalosporin drugs, vancomycin, gentamicin, ampicillin, and chloramphenicol are often effective. Often doctors prescribe combinations of these drugs to attack bacteria in different ways.

These medications are usually given intravenously in a hospital. In difficult cases they are given intrathecally or injected directly into the brain with a device called an Ommaya reservoir. Surgeons place this device under the scalp. It contains a supply of drugs that is slowly infused into the brain over a period of days or weeks.

As with sulfa and penicillin drugs, the antibiotics used to treat meningitis today work in different ways. Cefotaxime, for example, is a cephalosporin drug that prevents a wide range of bacteria from multiplying and from producing several proteins that make up the cell wall. Without a cell wall, the bacteria die. Gentamicin, which is one of the most powerful antibiotics, interferes with bacterial genes and causes bacteria to produce abnormal proteins that cannot keep them alive. It also damages bacterial cell walls.

Unfortunately, bacteria develop resistance to modern antibiotics just like they did to sulfa and penicillin drugs. Antibiotic resistance is one reason why 10 to 15 percent of the people with bacterial meningitis die today, even with treatment. Some of the powerful modern antibiotics like vancomycin can also have life-threatening side effects such as kidney failure or stroke. Patients with kidney failure may have to undergo kidney dialysis

The antibiotic cefotaxime (shown) is often used to treat meningitis, although it is sometimes ineffective because some bacteria have developed resistance to it and other antibiotics.

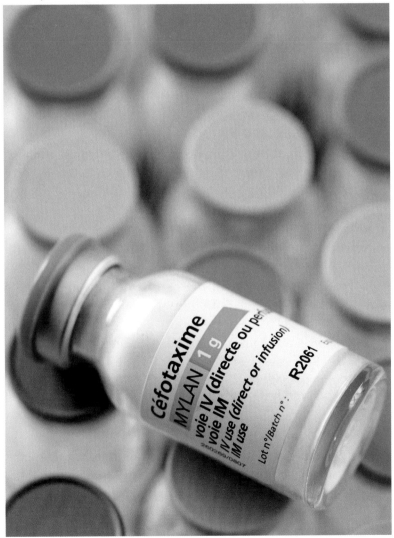

temporarily or permanently to perform the kidneys' essential job of cleansing toxins from the blood. Doctors must therefore carefully weigh the potential advantages and disadvantages of using these powerful drugs when the need arises.

In addition to using antibiotics, many physicians also start immediate treatment with corticosteroids like dexamethasone to reduce inflammation in the meninges. Dexamethasone is also used to treat other types of meningitis besides bacterial meningitis. Some experts claim it significantly reduces the chances of death and the incidence of long-term complications like hearing loss in survivors, but other scientists find dexamethasone not effective. Some believe it is most helpful in people with pneumococcal or Hib meningitis. Based on conflicting results, the authors of a 2010 study published in the journal *Lancet Neurology* concluded, "The benefit of adjunctive dexamethasone for all or any subgroups of patients with bacterial meningitis thus remains unproven."[25] However, dexamethasone is still widely used because many doctors believe it helps save lives.

The Importance of Prompt Treatment

One factor that has proved to influence survival in people with bacterial meningitis is how promptly patients are treated. The sooner treatment is started, the better the outcome. This is why doctors often begin antibiotic treatment with drugs that kill a wide range of bacteria before they determine exactly which bacteria are causing the illness. Once the bacteria are identified, doctors may switch to a drug that is more powerful against that pathogen, if necessary. This strategy has saved many lives. For example, a newborn named Paisley seemed to have a cold, but her doctor suspected meningitis and sent her to the hospital. There, her mother writes, "the doctors at the hospital took the strongest actions possible, assuming the worst case scenario and treating for meningitis before the tests had been processed. Their proactive playbook and prioritization of her case made a difference in a struggle where lost time can mean irreversible repercussions."[26]

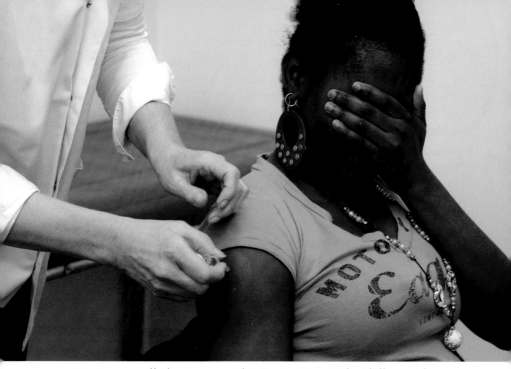

Doctors usually begin an antibiotic treatment that kills a wide range of bacteria before they determine which bacterium is causing the specific illness.

However, in many cases doctors do not test for meningitis in patients they believe have flu or a cold, and instead they send these patients home. Without treatment, the illness progresses rapidly to death. When families of patients who succumb to the disease find out that prompt treatment might have saved a loved one's life, this adds to the grief and frustration they are experiencing. A mother named Courtney, for example, lost her fourteen-month-old son after emergency room doctors sent him home because they thought he had flu. The child died twelve hours later. Knowing that prompt treatment might have saved him, Courtney wrote on the National Meningitis Association website, "I wish there was a way doctors had to check for meningitis every time a child went to the ER with flu like symptoms."[27]

Doctors, however, state that suspecting and treating for meningitis in every case that appears to be a cold or flu would be impractical and even dangerous. "Hospital wards would go into meltdown, the really sick children would have their treatments delayed and thousands of patients would be thrown into a panic with no need," writes pediatrician Sarah Jarvis. Jarvis and other physicians believe the best thing parents or other family members can do is to watch for worsening symptoms and return to a hospital if this happens: "When doctors reassure a parent that there are no worrying signs, they must always explain that there's no cause for concern *now*. . . . New symptoms should never be ignored."[28]

Other Treatments

Antibiotics are the main elements of treatment for bacterial meningitis, but patients may also receive other therapies, depending on individual symptoms and complications. These other treatments are also used in people with other types of meningitis. Pain and fever are treated with medications such as acetaminophen or prescription pain drugs. In cases where inflammation increases pressure in the brain, a catheter or shunt (tubes that drain fluid) may have to be inserted into the brain or frequent spinal taps must be performed to drain cerebrospinal fluid and reduce the pressure. Those who are expe-

The antifungal fluconazole is used to treat parasitic meningitis, but its effectiveness varies from patient to patient.

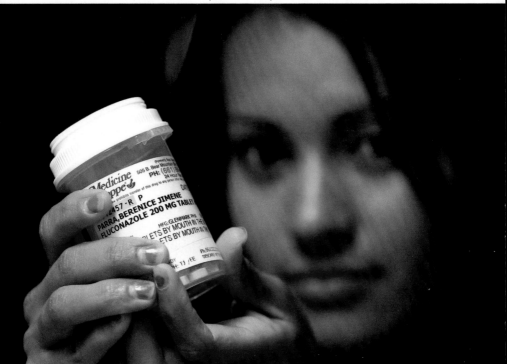

riencing seizures may be given sedatives or placed in a coma to stop the seizures. Those with breathing problems may be placed on a breathing tube and ventilator to keep them alive.

Besides these individualized therapies, treatment for non-bacterial meningitis depends on the cause. Many people with viral meningitis get better on their own without specific treatment. Those with severe disease are treated with medicine for pain and fever in a hospital, and those with mild cases are advised to stay home, rest, take pain medicine, and drink plenty of fluids. Some doctors prescribe the antiviral drug acyclovir, but it has not proved to be effective for meningitis.

Fungal meningitis is treated with high doses of antifungal medications such as amphotericin B, flucytosine, and fluconazole. These medications are known to pose significant risks of liver damage and neurological side effects such as hallucinations. For this reason, doctors do not prescribe them without confirming that a particular fungus is present. During the 2012 fungal meningitis outbreak, for example, the CDC issued warnings to doctors not to begin antifungal treatment unless clear evidence of infection was confirmed by laboratory tests.

Many times, treatment with antifungal drugs must continue for the rest of patients' lives because these medications control, but do not kill the infection. For cryptococcal infections, for example, doctors use amphotericin B, which is very powerful and very toxic, for two weeks and then switch to lifelong treatment with fluconazole, which is less dangerous. Fluconazole is one of the few antifungal drugs that can penetrate the blood-brain barrier.

Sometimes antifungals like amphotericin B and fluconazole are used to treat parasitic meningitis, but they are usually not effective. However, since meningitis caused by *Naegleria fowleri* and other parasites is usually fatal, physicians often try a variety of drugs that show some effect on parasites in a desperate attempt to save people's lives. Antifungal drugs have been combined with dexamethasone, the antibiotic ceftriaxone, and other drugs for this purpose. Only two people in the United States given these combinations have survived, and doctors are not sure whether any or all of the medications helped.

Kali Hardig, the girl who survived *Naegleria fowleri* meningitis in July 2013, was given a different experimental treatment. Doctors cooled her body down to 93.2°F (34°C) to reduce swelling in her brain. They also obtained permission to use a cancer drug called miltefosine that is approved for use in Germany but not in the United States. They chose miltefosine because it has proved to be effective against parasites similar to *Naegleria fowleri*. Hardig did recover after being in a coma and breathing with a ventilator for several weeks.

However, another child, Zachary Reyna of Florida, died in August 2013 after being given the same experimental treatment. Doctors are therefore unsure whether body cooling and/or miltefosine are truly effective. Physicians have tried using body cooling in other meningitis cases with no positive results. In one study published in the November 27, 2013, issue of the *Journal of the American Medical Association*, doctors at several hospitals in Paris, France, reported that patients with severe bacterial meningitis whose bodies were cooled to 89.6°F or 93.2°F (32°C or 34°C) for forty-eight hours were more likely to die than patients given conventional treatment. The researchers concluded, "Moderate hypothermia [body cooling] did not improve outcome in patients with severe bacterial meningitis and may even be harmful."[29] Clearly, further research is needed to assess the value of different degrees of body cooling in patients with different types of meningitis.

Treatment for Noninfectious Meningitis

As with infectious meningitis, treatment for noninfectious cases depends on the cause. The simplest treatment is for drug-induced meningitis—it involves stopping the drug that caused the disease. Most patients recover within about five days after the medication is discontinued.

On the other hand, treatment of malignant meningitis is rarely successful. Treatment usually consists of trying to relieve pain and neurological symptoms such as confusion with sedative drugs, along with injecting anticancer drugs directly into the brain and spinal cord. If the cancer cells are mostly confined to one area, radiation may also be administered to kill these cells.

Unfortunately, anticancer drugs can increase brain inflammation and worsen neurological symptoms, so many doctors choose not to administer them. Instead, they focus on making the patient as comfortable as possible during his or her remaining days. Patients with untreated malignant meningitis usually live from three to six weeks. Those who receive anticancer treatments usually live from three to sixteen weeks.

While treatment for malignant and parasitic meningitis is rarely successful, effective therapies have dramatically increased survival in people with other types of the disease. However, even meningitis survivors and their families face short- and long-term challenges that can significantly impact and alter their lives.

CHAPTER FOUR

Living with Meningitis

Living with any type of meningitis during the acute phase of the disease is painful and frightening for patients and their families, and often the challenges do not end when patients survive the infection. Many people spend weeks or even months in hospitals, and some spend even longer stretches in rehabilitation facilities to regain their strength and ability to function. For some individuals the mental and physical disabilities that result from the disease subside with time, while for others the impairments are permanent and drastically change their lives.

Short- and Long-Term Effects

The effects on everyday life start during the acute phase of the disease. Hospitalized adults cannot work or care for their families, and family members often must care for the person at home later on if he or she is disabled. Parents with hospitalized or disabled children may also not be able to return to work, and some children may not be able to resume going to school. This can lead to stress, financial difficulties, and practical challenges such as finding care for other children in the family.

The emotional toll on patients and families is also substantial. Patients describe the highly unpleasant nature of meningitis symptoms and hospital care as events that leave lasting physical and emotional scars. For instance, a woman named Sharon Cheslow writes that the headache she endured while ill with meningitis was something she will never forget: "The pressure against my skull was unbearable. It was the most excruciating physical pain I've ever felt in my life. Now, almost thirty years later, I cry thinking about this pain."[30] The unpleasant symptoms lead many meningitis survivors to have recurring nightmares and long-term problems with depression, anger, and anxiety. Many children also have problems with bed-wetting and temper tantrums after their ordeal.

For families, the emotional toll can be unbearable, especially when the patient is a child or young person. Maree Selwood, mother of meningitis survivor Adam Selwood, calls the day two-year-old Adam got sick "the most terrifying day of my life"[31] in an article on the Meningitis Centre of Australia website. She and her husband were frightened that Adam might die, and watching their son endure the pain and trauma of the disease and the medical procedures administered at the hospital was extremely difficult. Selwood describes what happened after doctors asked her and her husband to leave the room so they could perform a spinal tap: "We heard this high pitched scream come from the room; it broke my heart, my poor little baby, what could possibly be the matter with him? I was an emotional mess."[32]

Some meningitis sufferers cannot work or care for their families, and in some instances their families must later care for them at home.

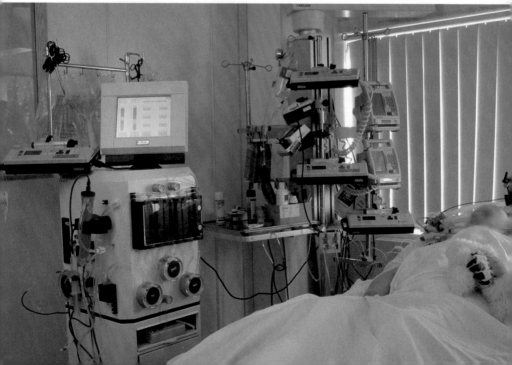

Adam Selwood

Adam Selwood was lucky to survive Hib meningitis when he was two years old in 1986. A prompt diagnosis and treatment made all the difference in his case. He was also lucky to recover completely and not to have permanent effects from the disease. In fact, he went on to become a professional athlete. He played Australian football for the Australian Football League's West Coast Eagles from 2003 to 2013, when he retired due to a back injury.

Selwood's gratitude for surviving meningitis led him to start helping the Meningitis Centre of Australia raise awareness of the disease in 2010. As the organization's ambassador, he educates the public about meningitis and offers support to families that have been affected. Selwood also participates in numerous events, such as World Meningitis Day each year on April 24, to bring attention to the toll meningitis takes on individuals and families. He told the Telethon Institute for Child Health Research: "Thanks to the quick actions of my parents and my doctor I was lucky to survive meningitis and make a full recovery. It's important that people are aware of the disease and know the signs and symptoms."

Quoted in Telethon Kids Institute. "Celebrating 20 Years of Meningitis Awareness," April 18, 2012. www.childhealthresearch.org.au/news-events/media-releases/2012/april/celebrating-20-years-of-meningitis-awareness.aspx.

Australian football player Adam Selwood survived meningitis when he was just two years old and is now a spokesman for the Meningitis Centre of Australia.

Adam's one-week hospitalization was an experience his family did not want to repeat, and fortunately, he recovered quickly. For Jane Danzi and her husband, however, the emotionally devastating ordeal when their five-month-old son, Cameron, had pneumococcal meningitis in 1996 went on and on. The ordeal began when she frantically rushed Cameron to a doctor after he became unconscious. Since they lived in a small town, they had to be flown to a regional hospital and then to a state hospital to receive care. Danzi and her husband spent ten days sitting by Cameron's bed in the intensive care unit and then two months in a hospital ward after he was able to breathe on his own. After weeks of watching Cameron endure ongoing seizures and other frightening events, they found out he had extensive brain damage that required ongoing physical and cognitive therapies. Danzi writes, "April 3, 1996 changed our lives forever, it is the day that we lost our hopes and dreams as first time parents and started a completely new journey."[33]

Losing a Loved One

The emotional trauma and life changes for families that lose a loved one, especially a child, to meningitis are even more intense. One mother whose daughter succumbed to meningococcal meningitis states, "It is the most horrible thing ever to bury a child."[34] Other parents echo this sentiment. Bob and Dee Dee Werner, who lost their college-aged daughter, Becky, write on the Confederation of Meningitis Organisations website, "On 25 February 2004 our healthy 20-year-old daughter, Becky, died unexpectedly from meningitis. Becky's death was, and continues to be, an unfathomable concept. We still cannot grasp the idea that she is gone and that we are facing the rest of our lives without her."[35] For some families, guilt over not seeking care soon enough to save a loved one's life worsens the impact of losing the individual. For example, Jimmy and Véronique of France write, "On account of our ignorance about meningitis, we lost our daughter Audrey."[36]

The grief of losing someone to meningitis extends beyond families to friends and communities. Sammy-Jo Farrell, whose college friend Tess succumbed to meningitis, writes, "I miss my best friend more every day and I always think of what she'd be doing now if she'd have survived that horrible disease."[37] Since infectious meningitis tends to strike college students who live in close dormitory quarters, the shock of losing a classmate reverberates throughout college communities. But this can in some ways be a good thing, since it results in increased awareness of meningitis and methods of preventing it.

Indeed, many families and friends of people affected by meningitis turn their grief and experiences into positive actions aimed at sparing others a similar fate. Many join local, national, or international support groups that help them cope and that also give them an opportunity to educate the public and assist others who are facing similar challenges. Jimmy and Véronique, for instance, founded the Association Audrey for this purpose and to raise funds for meningitis research. In a similar manner, Bob and Dee Dee Werner founded the Becky Werner Meningitis Foundation because, as they explain, "it became apparent that we needed to raise awareness of meningitis and spare other families the pain of burying their child or sibling at such a young and vibrant age."[38]

Dealing with Lasting Effects

Many families faced with ongoing disabilities in meningitis survivors also participate in meningitis organizations to obtain and offer support. Jane Danzi, whose son was left with significant mental and physical disabilities, derived great strength from the Meningitis Centre of Australia during her family's ordeal, and she now helps others facing similar obstacles. She writes, "We are now further along in our journey and have adapted to our different destination. Now I give support to other parents who are at the beginning of that tunnel and are searching for some light."[39]

Indeed, living through the acute illness is just the beginning of a lifetime of ongoing challenges faced by many meningitis survivors and their families. About 50 percent of survivors of bacterial meningitis have permanent brain damage and other

The pain of losing someone to meningitis extends beyond families to friends and even the community.

types of lasting effects, and many survivors of other types of meningitis experience ongoing effects as well. The most common areas of the brain to sustain damage are the hippocampus and cerebral cortex. The cerebral cortex is critical for many brain functions such as thinking, learning, speech, memory, and sensory and movement coordination. The hippocampus, which is located beneath the cerebral cortex, is also important in learning and memory.

Damage in these areas and weakness from lying in bed for extended periods lead to many of the long-term mental and physical problems in survivors, ranging from deafness to blindness to epilepsy to memory and movement deficits. Many people spend weeks or months in rehabilitation hospitals re-learning how to walk, talk, and perform other tasks after they recover from the acute illness. For some, this rehabilitation

Saving Lives

Bob and Dee Dee Werner founded the Becky Werner Meningitis Foundation to celebrate the life of their twenty-year-old
daughter, Becky, who died of meningitis in 2004, and to raise
awareness of the disease. The foundation educates the public
through a variety of programs and also raises funds for meningitis research. One of its programs involves Bob speaking to high
school students to inform them about symptoms, treatment,
and prevention. The Werners have received many accolades and
thank-yous from students and their families for these efforts.
One of the greatest tributes came from a high school student
named Molly Blum, who contracted meningitis shortly after one
of the presentations. Molly wrote a letter to thank the Werners
for saving her life, stating, "If you had not come to our school my
family and I would have just passed it as the flu. But I was persis-
tent and told my mom your story and immediately she took me
to the emergency room where I was then tested for meningitis
and it came back positive."

Quoted in Becky Werner Meningitis Foundation. "School Presentations." www
.stampoutmeningitis.com/schools.htm.

takes even longer or does not eliminate all the aftereffects.
An October 2013 National Public Radio report about people
affected by the 2012 fungal meningitis outbreak in the United
States, for example, revealed that a year after the outbreak,
many patients were still undergoing physical therapy to regain
their strength and ability to walk. In some patients the infection had spread to the arachnoid mater in areas of the spinal
cord that regulate bladder function, leading to chronic pain
and urine retention. Many of the patients were also still taking intravenous antifungal drugs at home a year after being
released from the hospital. Many had relapsed (experienced a

recurrence of infection after being free of it) and had to begin treatment again.

No matter what type of meningitis a patient recovers from, in some instances some or all of the aftereffects diminish over time. A patient named Keith McIntyre, for example, describes his journey with bacterial meningitis on the Meningitis Foundation of America website:

> When I first came out of the coma, I could not concentrate long enough to even watch a movie. That gradually improved and I was soon able to handle simple tasks at work. But for years, at 3 to 6 month intervals it seemed like a door would open in my brain and I suddenly could do something that I didn't know I could do before. It was as if my brain was gradually re-wiring itself around the damaged areas.[40]

The physical effects for McIntyre, however, did not subside. He has no feeling in his feet, poor balance, and uses a wheelchair or walks with a walker. He also has hearing loss and breathing problems.

A patient named Scott Madsen, on the other hand, found that the mental and physical aftereffects of having bacterial meningitis at age twenty-seven kept worsening over time. His ongoing problems include worsening memory lapses, uncontrollable shaking in his hands, severe nerve damage in his hands and feet, advanced arthritis in his back, chronic fatigue syndrome, and frequent bouts of pneumonia. Doctors are not sure why some seriously ill patients recover more or less completely than others do. This seems to depend partly on which parts of the brain and the rest of the body were affected by the meningitis and partly on the patient's age.

Age Differences in Lasting Effects

Although any meningitis survivor may be faced with ongoing effects, several studies have found that these lasting problems tend to be more serious in adults than in children. Infectious disease specialist Robert Read of the University of

Southampton in England explains in a *Daily Mail* article that this is because

the adult immune system tends to react far more aggressively to the infection. It's thought that this occurs because adults tolerate larger numbers of bacteria in their bloodstream before their immune system kicks in. And when it does, the response is very powerful. This leads to the release of chemicals called cytokines, which, though they help cells of the immune system "talk" to each other, also have the side-effect of producing general inflammation in critical parts of the body, such as the brain as well as blood vessels.[41]

The case of Tyler Green, who had pneumococcal meningitis as an infant, supports the contention that babies and children who survive have a greater chance of avoiding lasting effects. Doctors put Tyler into a coma to stop the many seizures he was having, and they told his parents he had a very slim chance of surviving because the strain of bacteria he had was resistant to antibiotics. Still, they administered a powerful combination of vancomycin and rifampin to try to save the boy's life. Two days later Tyler woke up. Although his doctors warned his parents that he would have lasting physical and cognitive defects, when he was seven his father described him as a straight-A student and an outstanding athlete.

Even though children are less likely to experience serious lasting effects, many of them do have ongoing physical and mental deficiencies. In some cases the reasons for this are unknown, but a study by Danish researchers reported in April 2013 revealed that with bacterial meningitis, the particular bacteria that cause the infection play a role. The researchers found that infection with pneumococcal or Hib meningitis during childhood often led to lower educational achievement, less chance of attending college, and less economic self-sufficiency as adults in people in all economic classes. A childhood infection with meningococcal meningitis, on the other hand, could also lead to these consequences, but usually did so in children who lived in impoverished homes. The investigators concluded that the amount of intellectual stimulation and encouragement that children in more affluent households received played a role in bolstering their academic success after surviving meningococcal meningitis, but not Hib or pneumococcal meningitis. They believe this may mean that different bacteria lead to different forms of brain damage.

Attitude and Coping

Although the type and seriousness of a meningitis infection play a role in determining its long-term effects, emotional factors such as a positive attitude and a determination to lead a fulfilling life also influence the outcome for both children and adults. Andy Marso, for instance, almost died from meningococcal meningitis when he was a college student. Doctors had to amputate his fingers and toes because gangrene set in, and he was unable to stand up for a year. He finally learned to walk with leg braces and realized that he could accomplish many things if he tried hard enough. He earned his college degree and went on to help others with meningitis by raising awareness of the disease. One of his accomplishments was writing and publishing a book titled *Worth the Pain: How Meningitis Nearly Killed Me—Then Changed My Life for the Better.* In the book, he writes about how surviving meningitis opened a new, more meaningful life for him. In his words, "My first life ended on April 27, 2004."[42]

Many other meningitis survivors have also forged ahead and made the best of less-than-ideal situations. Mike LaForgia, whose right leg and part of his left foot were amputated, learned to run marathons with his artificial limbs. Nick Springer, who lost both hands and legs to meningitis, competes in wheelchair rugby and helps disabled children and adults learn to get around with wheelchairs. A young man named Blake Schuchardt was on kidney dialysis for more than a year after surviving bacterial meningitis and had to have a kidney transplant. He also lost three toes. After he recovered, he attended nursing school and now works as a home therapy dialysis nurse, teaching patients to perform dialysis at home. He writes, "I want to show those who are currently going through meningitis or dialysis that their life is not over and they can do anything they put their minds to."[43]

Not all survivors are able to overcome the difficulties posed by meningitis, however. Many remain depressed, anxious, or in severe physical pain. Ashley Mason, who had bacterial men-

In his book *Worth the Pain*, Andy Marso writes about his near-death experience from a bout of meningitis.

ingitis at age seven, is one individual who still struggles. As a child, she had most of one foot and half of her other leg amputated. She also had additional surgeries over the next thirteen years to graft skin and muscle tissue to her leg to relieve some of the ongoing pain. She writes on the National Meningitis Association website, "I am in constant pain and almost 20 years old. I got sick almost thirteen years ago, and I'm still trying to figure out how to deal with the effects of meningitis."[44]

One thing that meningitis survivors and their families agree about is the importance of educating the public about the fact that many cases can be prevented with vaccinations and other preventive measures. Worldwide efforts to enhance prevention have intensified in recent years to keep as many people as possible from suffering from this life-changing disease.

CHAPTER FIVE

Preventing Meningitis

Even though many people today survive a bout with meningitis, the disease continues to kill and disable hundreds of thousands of individuals each year. Meningitis advocacy groups and public health officials therefore advocate preventing the disease as preferable to relying on treatments to save lives. As Sumaiya Khan writes in a *Buzzle* article, "Prevention is indeed better than cure!"[45]

The Road to Vaccinations

One of the most effective methods of preventing contagious diseases caused by bacteria or viruses is vaccination. Vaccines are drugs that stimulate the immune system to defend the body against a microorganism without making an individual sick. The immunized individual is then resistant to becoming ill if later exposed to the microorganism.

Doctors were familiar with the concept of introducing a disease-causing pathogen into people to trigger an immune response long before the first real vaccines were developed. One of the most dreaded infectious diseases throughout history was smallpox. Until the late 1700s doctors and laypeople in many places injected pus from smallpox skin lesions into healthy people to prevent them from getting the disease. This practice was known as variolation, since the virus that causes smallpox is called variola. One major problem with variolation was that it often killed people. But many people chose to undergo the procedure because the death rate from variolation was much lower than that from actually contracting smallpox.

At the end of the eighteenth century, the British doctor Edward Jenner made a discovery that changed the history of vaccination. Jenner (and many others) was aware that milkmaids did not usually get smallpox because they were exposed to the closely related cowpox virus when they milked cows. Cowpox did not make people sick but did elicit an immune response.

British physician Edward Jenner inoculates people with a vaccine he developed for smallpox. It was the first use of vaccination in medical history.

Jenner used this principle to experiment with deliberately introducing cowpox virus into people to give them immunity to smallpox. The procedure was effective, and Jenner called it "vaccination" because the term *vacca* means "cow" in Latin and the term *vaccinia* means "cowpox." According to an article in *Baylor University Medical Center Proceedings*, "Jenner's work represented the first scientific attempt to control an infectious disease by the deliberate use of vaccination."[46]

Vaccine Improvements

Vaccinations for smallpox and other diseases were soon used in many places. In 1879 Louis Pasteur advanced vaccination safety when he developed a technique for attenuating, or weakening, viruses and bacteria before using them in vaccines. This involved heating the microorganisms without killing them. Attenuated microorganisms are still capable of provoking an immune response, but they cannot cause disease. This meant that scientists could now use dangerous pathogens like smallpox in vaccines rather than rely on similar but less dangerous microorganisms such as cowpox viruses.

This discovery gave scientists some of the tools needed to develop a meningitis vaccine. The first meningitis-causing bacterium that was targeted was *Neisseria meningitidis*. However, inducing an immune response to a meningococcus vaccine turned out to be difficult because of the bacterium's protective polysaccharide capsule. In the 1930s researchers made progress in this regard when they discovered that grinding up and purifying the capsule before putting it into a vaccine allowed the immune system to identify and create antibodies to the bacterium. Researchers also found that different strains of meningococci had different types of polysaccharide coatings that provoked the formation of different types of antibodies. This offered a method of selectively targeting different bacterial strains with vaccines made of different polysaccharides.

The U.S. government established several commissions to fund vaccine research for meningitis and other infectious diseases in an effort to protect soldiers before they were sent to fight overseas in World War II (1941–1945). The Commission on Meningitis funded studies at Columbia University, where a team of scientists developed and tested a new polysaccharide vaccine. However, the vaccine was not effective enough to warrant manufacturing it.

When new antibiotics proved to treat bacterial meningitis effectively in the early 1940s, research on vaccines was halted. But after meningococci and other bacteria started developing resistance to these antibiotics, interest in finding effective vaccines revived. During the 1960s, researchers led by Malcolm Artenstein at the Walter Reed Army Institute of Research developed new methods of creating a polysaccharide vaccine for types A and C meningococci, which were causing many outbreaks at army bases. The team conducted clinical trials involving thousands of people. They randomly administered either the vaccine or a placebo (fake) to volunteers in experimental and control groups to determine whether the vaccine, rather than the expectation of success, would truly protect people from meningitis. This vaccine proved to be extremely safe and effective, and the U.S. military began immunizing all its personnel. According to Artenstein's son, Andrew W. Artenstein, an infectious disease expert and author of *In the Blink of an Eye*, the new vaccine "virtually eliminated this pathogen as a health problem in the military."[47]

Other Meningitis Vaccines

Other scientists soon developed modified meningococcal vaccines that included polysaccharides from four of the most common bacterial strains. This type of vaccine is known as a quadrivalent vaccine. In the 1980s doctors began administering quadrivalent vaccines to people at high risk for meningitis—military people, college students living in dormitories, and people traveling to places where the disease was common.

Research on meningitis vaccines continued, in part because the quadrivalent vaccines proved to be ineffective in babies under age two. During the 1970s several independent teams of researchers made progress in finding ways to elicit an immune response in babies and young children whose immune systems are just "learning" to combat pathogens. One effective technique involved linking polysaccharide molecules to a protein. This type of vaccine is called a conjugate vaccine since it is created by linking (conjugating) several molecules. Conjugate vaccines are more likely to elicit antibody production because they stimulate more than one element of the immune system.

One of the first effective conjugate vaccines was for Hib bacteria, which caused many cases of meningitis in babies and young children. Scientists attached a Hib polysaccharide to proteins taken from a toxin made by diphtheria bacteria to make this vaccine. It was effective in causing babies' immune systems to produce Hib antibodies, and during the 1990s the Hib conjugate vaccine became one of the many vaccines routinely given to babies in the United States. It practically elimi-

The first effective conjugate vaccine was the Hib vaccine. The Hib bacterium had caused a multitude of cases of meningitis in babies and young children.

nated Hib in this country and others that began using it. Before the vaccine was introduced, about twenty thousand children under age five in the United States became ill with Hib meningitis each year, and about one thousand died.

Scientists started making conjugate meningococcal vaccines as well. They continued to improve these vaccines by using polysaccharides from multiple strains of the bacteria and linking them to proteins that elicited even stronger immune responses. In 2005 a quadrivalent conjugate meningococcal vaccine (MenACWY-D) was licensed for routine use in adolescents and as an optional vaccine for children and adults up to age fifty-five at risk for contracting meningococcal meningitis. The vaccine was not effective in babies, however, and it was not until 2012 that the FDA licensed the first meningococcal vaccine for use in infants. It is called Hib-MenCY-TT because it protects against Hib and type C and Y meningococci.

Vaccines against pneumococcal bacteria are also available. The conjugate PCV13 vaccine protects against thirteen of ninety known strains of pneumococci, and the polysaccharide PPSV23 vaccine protects against twenty-three strains. PCV13 is routinely given to babies, and PPSV23 is recommended for people over age sixty-five and for children and adults with chronic health problems and those with cochlear implants that help them hear (cochlear implants increase the risk of meningitis). Pneumococcal vaccines have cut the number of cases of pneumococcal meningitis in the United States by about 80 percent.

Side Effects and Boosters

Public health experts have determined that meningitis vaccines' positive effects are significant enough to recommend widespread vaccination, even though some side effects have been reported. Although all vaccines can have side effects, studies have shown that side effects from meningitis vaccines are usually mild. Up to 50 percent of people who receive MenACWY-D or PPSV23, for example, have a bit of pain and swelling at the injection site, mild fever, dizziness, headache, or nausea. Rarely, serious allergies, seizures, other serious effects, or even death occur.

Shortly after MenACWY-D was approved in 2005, several cases of people developing Guillain-Barré syndrome (GBS) after injection were reported. This raised public apprehension about the vaccine. GBS is a disorder that involves paralysis (usually temporary) after the immune system attacks nerves. Public health officials issued a warning that people who had previously experienced GBS should not receive the vaccination. However, in 2010 this warning was canceled when, according to the CDC, evidence indicated that "the potential small increased risk for GBS post-MenACWY-D vaccination was outweighed by the protection that the vaccine offers against meningococcal disease."[48]

In addition to carefully monitoring the incidence of side effects from vaccines during clinical trials and after vaccines are licensed for public use, public health officials also conduct tests to determine how well people's immune systems respond to the vaccines. Technicians take blood samples and measure serum antibodies to assess whether or not an individual produces enough antibodies to provide protection from illness if the person is later exposed to the pathogen. This type of test is called an antibody titer.

Studies show that vaccinated individuals' antibody titers for meningitis vaccines decline over time. For example, a 2012 study found that antibody titers in 82 percent of adolescents vaccinated with MenACWY-D were high enough to prevent disease less than one year after vaccination. This percentage dropped to 80 percent between one and two years after vaccination, 71 percent between two and three years, and 59 percent between three and six years. This is why agencies such as the CDC recommend that people receive booster doses of this type of vaccine three or more years after the initial vaccination.

Herd Immunity and Opposition to Vaccinations

Vaccines do not just protect people who receive them from certain diseases. They also lead to herd, or community, immunity. Herd immunity occurs when most people in a community are vaccinated, and as a result, fewer unvaccinated people

Vaccines for Meningitis

There are several vaccines for bacterial meningitis available:

- The meningococcal quadrivalent polysaccharide vaccine is approved for use as a single dose in people older than two.
- The quadrivalent meningococcal conjugate vaccine is available in two forms: MenACWY-D, approved as a single dose for people aged two to fifty-five and in two doses for children aged nine to twenty-three months; and MenACWY-CRM, approved for single-dose use in people two to fifty-five years old.
- Hib-MenCY-TT protects against Hib and two strains of meningococci. It is approved for use in four doses for children aged six weeks through eighteen months. Adults with AIDS or sickle-cell anemia or whose spleen has been removed also receive this vaccine.
- The pneumococcal conjugate vaccine (PCV13) is routinely given to children under age two and is recommended for children two to five years old with cancer, chronic heart or lung disease, or cochlear implants.
- The pneumococcal polysaccharide vaccine (PPSV23) is given to older children and adults who are at risk of getting pneumococcal disease or who are over age sixty-five.

contract a contagious disease. For example, after widespread childhood immunizations with meningitis vaccines began in the United States, the numbers of unvaccinated adults getting bacterial meningitis declined gradually. A 2011 study concluded, "Herd immunity accounts for ~50% of the protection by meningococcal serogroup C PPCVs, pneumococcal PPCV7, and *H. influenzae* b PPCVs."[49] Herd immunity is especially important for individuals who cannot receive certain immunizations because they are pregnant, have some immune disorders, or are too young. Some vaccinations, for instance, are not approved for babies under six months, one year, or two years old.

However, public health experts are concerned that herd immunity for some diseases that were once eradicated in the United States is disappearing because many parents are refusing to allow their children to be vaccinated. Many of these parents have concerns about reports that vaccines can cause autism and other diseases. In response, public health agencies like the CDC and the World Health Organization have presented studies that prove vaccines do not cause autism or other diseases and have argued that the risks of not receiving vaccinations outweigh the risks of receiving them. But many people still are not being vaccinated, and for the first time in decades, outbreaks of previously eradicated contagious diseases such as whooping cough and measles are occurring in the United States and Europe. Experts fear this could happen with forms of meningitis that have been mostly eliminated by vaccines if many people refuse to be vaccinated.

The antivaccine movement has caused the reappearance of some diseases that had been eradicated in the United States due to vaccinations.

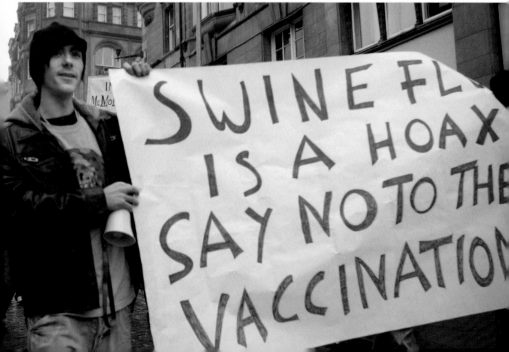

Additional Preventive Measures

In addition to receiving vaccines, other ways of preventing most forms of bacterial meningitis include taking preventive antibiotics after being exposed to an infected person, avoiding close contact, and not sharing food and eating utensils. Frequent hand washing also helps keep bacteria from getting into the nose or mouth. To prevent meningitis caused by *Listeria monocytogenes* bacteria, which spread through contaminated food, experts recommend thoroughly washing raw fruits and vegetables before cutting, cooking, or eating them. This includes scrubbing the peels of produce such as melons that will be peeled. It is also important to keep produce away from uncooked meats and poultry and to wash knives, cutting boards, countertops, and hands with hot water and soap before handling produce. All meats and poultry should be thoroughly cooked before eating.

Listeria can also grow in refrigerators. It is less likely to grow if the temperature is kept at 40°F (4.4°C) or lower. The CDC also recommends cleaning any spills or raw meat drips in the refrigerator with a disinfectant. It cautions against eating any foods past their expiration date and advises people to avoid raw, unpasteurized milk and related products, such as Mexican cheeses.

There are no vaccines for viral meningitis, and preventive measures include avoiding close contact, not sharing food or eating utensils, and frequent hand washing, especially after changing diapers or using the toilet. To help prevent viral meningitis caused by mosquito-borne illnesses like West Nile virus, experts advise wearing insect repellant to avoid being bitten by mosquitoes. Meningitis caused by LCMV can be prevented by avoiding contact with rodents and keeping pet rodents away from wild rodents. The CDC also recommends washing hands thoroughly after caring for pet rodents and disinfecting areas touched by wild rodents if they get into a house.

The only way individuals can prevent most types of fungal meningitis is to avoid being around soil that contains certain fungi. The CDC recommends that people with weak immune systems stay away from bird droppings and avoid digging in soil in areas where *Histoplasma, Coccidioides,* or *Blastomyces* fungi live. A report by the FDA also points out that the 2012 fungal meningitis outbreak could have been prevented—not by the individuals who were sickened—if public health agencies had more carefully monitored compounding pharmacies like the New England Compounding Center. This facility and others have been shut down, and new laws allow the FDA to monitor similar businesses carefully in hopes of preventing similar outbreaks.

Increasing Meningitis Vaccine Awareness

Some people do not receive vaccinations because they are not aware of their availability. Others do not believe they are at risk for certain diseases. About 30 percent of teenagers in the United States are not vaccinated against meningococcal disease for these reasons. Lynn Bozof of the National Meningitis Association states in a HealthDay article that many college students in particular erroneously believe they do not need vaccinations because they are young and healthy. She encourages young people to get vaccinated because, in her words, "my son was a young, healthy 20-year-old. And he died of meningitis."[1]

Like Bozof, many other parents of young people who have succumbed to meningitis encourage teenagers to receive vaccinations. For the parents of Nicolis Williams of Texas, the tragedy of losing their son in February 2011 was compounded by the fact that Nicolis was not vaccinated against meningococcal disease because of a technicality. Nicolis's father, Greg, writes, "It was only after our son died from meningitis that we learned there was a vaccine to prevent this devastating disease. Our grief became unbearable when we discovered that Nicolis had not been required to be vaccinated because he didn't live in a dorm."[2] Nicolis's parents worked with advocacy groups to encourage Texas lawmakers

Preventing parasitic meningitis involves avoiding places where disease-causing parasites live. The CDC states, "The only certain way to prevent a *Naegleria fowleri* infection is to refrain from water-related activities in or with warm, untreated, or poorly-treated water."[50] For individuals who wish to swim in warm ponds or lakes, the CDC suggests wearing nose plugs, not stirring up soil on lake bottoms, and not entering the water when temperatures are particularly high or water levels

to pass the Jamie Schanbaum/Nicolis Williams Act in late 2011. This law now requires all new college students in Texas to be vaccinated against meningitis.

1. Quoted in Amy Norton. "As More Meningitis Cases Hit Colleges, Experts Urge Awareness." HealthDay, November 26, 2013. http://consumer.healthday.com /kids-health-information-23/adolescents-and-teen-health-news-719/as-more -meningitis-cases-hit-colleges-experts-urge-awareness-682523.html.

2. Greg Williams. "Greg's Story." Confederation of Meningitis Organisations. www .comomeningitis.org/personal-meningitis-stories/gregs-story.

Lynn Bozof founded the National Meningitis Foundation to raise awareness of the disease that killed her son.

To prevent meningitis caused by *Listeria monocytogenes* bacteria in food, thorough washing of raw vegetables and fruits is recommended.

are low. To prevent infection when irrigating clogged nasal passages, the CDC recommends using only sterilized water.

Preventive measures for all types of meningitis have reduced the incidence of the disease in many places. In the future, health experts hope new methods of prevention will further reduce the impact of this deadly disease.

CHAPTER SIX

The Future

Even with improvements in diagnosis, treatment, and prevention of meningitis, experts agree there is still much to be accomplished before all types of meningitis can be conquered. Many people today die or are disabled due to delayed diagnosis. Existing treatments are often ineffective, and preventive vaccines do not exist for all forms of the disease. Much research is therefore being conducted in hopes that meningitis will be better contained and managed in the future.

Research into Diagnosis

Early detection of the disease is one area that meningitis experts believe needs improvement. "Health professionals involved in recognition and early management of serious illness should receive training to recognise the signs and symptoms of meningitis,"[51] states the Meningitis Research Foundation. Meningitis research and advocacy organizations are therefore helping health-care professionals design training materials to help doctors make quick diagnoses so treatment can be started immediately if necessary.

In addition to focusing on educating doctors, researchers are looking for methods of quickly diagnosing meningitis with laboratory tests. Michael Cooperstock of the University of Missouri School of Medicine, for instance, recently found an accurate way to screen for early-stage bacterial meningitis. Most physicians look for increases in the total number of white blood cells in the blood as evidence of a bacterial infection. However, in a study reported in October 2013, Cooperstock revealed that more than one-third of patients with bacterial meningitis do not have elevated total white blood cell counts. This means that doctors who only look at total white blood cell counts would not diagnose a bacterial infection in these patients.

Cooperstock also found that most patients with bacterial meningitis have abnormal quantities and qualities of a specific type of white blood cell called neutrophils. He states in a news article, "When we looked at the neutrophil counts of each patient, we examined not only the total number of neutrophils, but also the number of immature neutrophils and the ratio of immature to total neutrophil cells. We found that 94 percent of the patients showed an abnormality in one or more of these three tests, indicating that a serious infection might be present."[52] The research team believes that relying on a detailed neutrophil test would allow doctors to determine quickly that bacterial meningitis is likely to be present, even before a spinal tap and bacterial identification are completed. Doctors could then hospitalize and start antibiotics in patients who otherwise might have been sent home.

Other researchers are focusing on improving diagnosis of specific types of bacterial meningitis. One such type that kills many people, particularly in developing countries, is tuberculous meningitis. This is caused by the bacteria responsible for tuberculosis lung infections. According to researchers at Xijing Hospital in China, "Early and reliable diagnosis of tuberculous meningitis (TBM) still poses a great challenge"[53] because the bacteria are not visible in patients' cerebrospinal fluid during the early stages of infection. These bacteria cannot be seen, because white blood cells called macrophages immediately surround and ingest them when they enter the cerebrospinal fluid. The Chinese research team has developed a laboratory test called early secretory antigenic target-6 (ESAT-6) that can detect tuberculous bacteria inside macrophages. The team is now studying how reliable ESAT-6 is for early diagnosis of tuberculous meningitis.

A microbiologist holds an analytical profile index test panel that shows a color code for a specific bacterium that causes meningitis—in this case, *Listeria monocytogenes.*

Improving Treatment for Bacterial Meningitis

While research on methods of early diagnosis seeks to improve treatment outcome by allowing doctors to start treatment immediately, other current research focuses on improving treatment with new drugs or new uses for existing drugs. One problem with many antibiotics used to treat bacterial meningitis is that they can contribute to the permanent brain damage seen in many survivors. This is especially true for antibiotics such as ceftriaxone, which kills bacteria by causing them to burst. Pieces of the bacteria then lodge in the subarachnoid spaces of the meninges, exacerbating the inflammation that leads to brain damage. Researchers at University Hospital Inselspital in Berne, Switzerland, explain that even when dexamethasone is administered to diminish inflammation, "children are particularly vulnerable to this form of brain damage because of ongoing development of neurological functions."[54]

Studies on baby rats indicate that administering an antibiotic called daptomycin with ceftriaxone reduces brain inflammation caused by the latter. Daptomycin does not cause bacteria to burst. Instead, it kills them by causing tiny channels to open in the outer membranes. This allows chemicals needed for growth to leak out. The Swiss researchers are testing whether the daptomycin-ceftriaxone combination effectively reduces inflammation in children with bacterial meningitis. They are also assessing whether reducing the amount of inflammation diminishes brain damage.

In other research on preventing brain damage, investigators at Hospital Universitari de Bellvitge in Spain are testing whether the drug phenytoin prevents seizures in adults with pneumococcal meningitis. Many patients currently experience seizures that result in permanent brain damage. Phenytoin is used to treat a variety of seizure disorders and is often given after brain surgery to prevent seizures. It works by diminishing abnormal electrical activity in the brain. However, phenytoin is

Studies on rats have shown that treatment with the antibiotic daptomycin combined with the antibiotic ceftriaxone reduces brain inflammation caused by ceftriaxone.

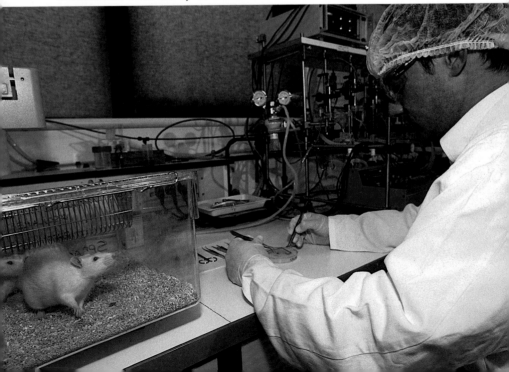

known to interact adversely with other drugs. Doctors do not know how it will interact with the antibiotics and corticosteroids used to treat bacterial meningitis, and the current study seeks answers to these questions.

Research into Other Meningitis Treatments

Since bacterial meningitis kills more people than other types of meningitis do, much research is directed at improving treatments for this form of the disease. However, researchers are aware that improvements are also needed in treating other types of meningitis. Scientists at the University of Liverpool in England note that viral meningitis "has been relatively neglected in terms of research. However, it is still an important cause of illness. Some patients that recover from [viral] meningitis keep having further attacks (relapses) for years ahead; others have memory and concentration problems."[55] These investigators plan to test the antiviral drug acyclovir in people with viral meningitis caused by herpes viruses. First they are doing a study to determine how many cases are caused by these viruses. They suspect that herpes viruses are responsible for many more cases than are reported. Since acyclovir has been shown to effectively treat other diseases caused by herpes, they believe it may have widespread applications in treating viral meningitis if it proves to be effective.

Other research is focused on finding effective treatments for the 99 percent fatal primary amoebic meningoencephalitis. One drug being tested is the cancer drug miltefosine. This was the experimental drug given to Kali Hardig in 2013. Although Hardig survived, other meningitis patients given this drug have died. Researchers therefore seek to determine scientifically whether or not miltefosine is effective for this purpose. Scientists in South Korea found that miltefosine is more effective than amphotericin B in killing *Naegleria fowleri* amoebas in test tubes and in mice, and current studies are being conducted with humans.

Like parasitic meningitis, fungal meningitis is often fatal, so researchers are testing new treatments to help save lives. One study at the University of Minnesota is testing the safety and effectiveness of adding the antidepressant sertraline (commonly marketed as Zoloft) to conventional treatment with fluconazole in treating cryptococcal meningitis in humans. This study began after scientists at Texas A&M University reported in 2012 that sertraline kills cryptococci in test tubes and eradicates cryptococcal infections in mice. The Texas A&M study, in turn, was motivated by physicians' reports that female patients taking sertraline for depression found that the drug cleared up vaginal fungal infections caused by candida. The Texas A&M scientists reasoned that sertraline might also be effective against cryptococcal fungi, and their experiments showed that the drug does indeed prevent cryptococci from manufacturing proteins needed to stay alive. Since sertraline penetrates the blood-brain barrier and is safe for long-term use, the Texas A&M scientists realized it might be useful in eradicating fungal meningitis. They write that "the data demonstrate that sertraline alone is efficacious [effective] against cryptoccosis and that the combination of sertraline with fluconazole is a more effective treatment than either drug alone"[56] in mice.

In another fungal meningitis study, the CDC commissioned the University of Alabama–Birmingham to study the effects of various treatments on the long-term outcome in about five hundred survivors of the 2012 fungal meningitis outbreak. The researchers are investigating which treatments were most effective in saving lives, what side effects they have, how long treatment should continue, and how often patients relapse after certain treatments. According to the CDC, "This information will be used to improve the care of current patients and any future patients linked to this outbreak, and potentially can inform treatment decisions in future cases of meningitis caused by similar types of fungal organisms."[57]

Research into Causes

Testing and analyzing new medications is only one strategy researchers use to try to improve meningitis treatment. Another method involves studying how and why certain micro-

Clinical Trial Phases

The FDA in the United States and comparable agencies in other countries require drug manufacturers to conduct extensive clinical trials to test the safety and effectiveness of new drugs and new uses for existing drugs. After drugs are found to be safe and effective in laboratory animals, three phases of clinical trials in human volunteers are required. Phase 1 trials test a drug on a small group of about twenty patients to establish safe and effective doses. In Phase 2 the drug is tested on a larger group of approximately one hundred people. Phase 3 involves testing on thousands of patients divided into experimental and control groups. Those in experimental groups are given the drug being tested. Those in control groups are unknowingly given a fake (placebo) that looks like the real thing. This helps researchers determine whether any perceived positive effects are due to the drug itself or to the expectation of success. Experimental drugs may be approved for widespread use only after all three phases are completed and results show that the drug's advantages outweigh any adverse effects.

organisms cause the disease and why some people get sick after being exposed to these microorganisms while others do not. As an example, in 2013 scientists led by Michael Jennings at Griffith University made an important breakthrough when they discovered how meningococci attach themselves to peoples' airways. The researchers found that these bacteria use arm-like structures called pili to attach themselves to receptors (called platelet activating factor receptors) on cells in the lining of the airways. This process begins after pili identify certain proteins on the surface of these cells. Understanding how this occurs could eventually lead to new treatments and methods of preventing meningitis by interfering with the attachment process. The researchers plan to conduct additional studies as well to determine how the bacteria proceed to cross

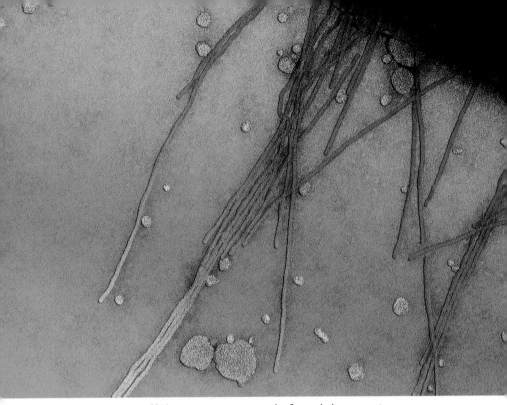

Scientists at Griffith University recently found that meningococcus bacteria have pili, or long strands (shown), with which they attach themselves to cells in the lining of the airways.

the blood-brain barrier after attaching to the airways in some individuals but not in others.

Other researchers are focusing on how genetic factors affect susceptibility and meningococcal disease severity. A team at Imperial College London has collected DNA samples from thousands of people who have or have not been affected by meningococcal meningitis. They are using genome scanning methods to look for genes and gene mutations that appear consistently in people who have had the disease. A genome is an organism's complete set of DNA. Thus far, the investigators have found that mutations in a gene called the complement factor H gene makes people more likely to become ill when exposed to meningococci. These mutations also make people more susceptible to sepsis from meningococcal meningitis. The complement factor H gene regulates the immune system's production of cells and chemicals that cause inflammation. "Excessive complement action, may in part be responsible for the multisystem failures seen in sepsis,"[58] the researchers conclude. Further studies to determine exactly how these mutations affect the immune system are under way.

In other gene studies, researchers funded by the National Institute of Allergy and Infectious Diseases seek to determine why previously healthy people sometimes develop cryptococcal meningitis, which usually affects those with impaired immune systems. These scientists suspect that mutations in several genes may direct the immune systems of these individuals to produce abnormally low numbers of a type of white blood cell called DC4 cells. However, they have not yet pinpointed these mutations.

Research into Prevention

Doctors may someday be able to prevent meningitis by correcting gene mutations that make people susceptible. In the meantime, vaccinations are the best method of preventing some forms of the disease. However, vaccines are not yet available for some types of meningitis, and some areas in the world do not have access to existing vaccines because of their cost. Research into developing new vaccines and projects to increase access are therefore ongoing.

Access to vaccines has been particularly limited in the meningitis belt of Africa. In 2001 the World Health Organization organized a committee to devise methods of making effective, inexpensive vaccines available in this region. Several international agencies collaborated with vaccine manufacturers to reach this goal through a project called the Meningitis Vaccine Project. Scientists involved in the project produced a vaccine called MenAfriVac® (meningococcal type A conjugate vaccine) and tested it in children and young adults. They found it to be safe, effective, and inexpensive at under fifty cents per dose.

MenAfriVac® was approved for use in 2009. The first country to authorize widespread vaccination of people aged one to twenty-nine was Burkina Faso. In December 2010 more than 11.4 million children in that country were vaccinated. Other African countries followed suit, and by 2012 about 55 million people had been vaccinated. The Meningitis Vaccine Project aims to vaccinate an additional 265 million people in Africa by 2016.

A 2013 study found that the incidence of type A meningococcal meningitis declined significantly after these vaccinations began. In Niger alone, type A bacteria previously caused 98.6 percent of meningococcal infections. By 2011 this had declined to 26.4 percent. However, as the number of type A infections declined, the number of type W infections increased from 72.2 percent in 2010 to 97.8 percent in 2011. The researchers concluded that "whereas large outbreaks of A should be eliminated by widespread deployment of the conjugate A vaccine, it is not yet clear how the other serogroups, in particular W, will evolve in response to this new situation."[59] The researchers suggest that low-cost vaccines that include more meningococcal strains may be necessary to address this issue.

Type B Meningococcal Vaccines

Meningococcal vaccines in areas of the world other than Africa are generally effective against type W bacteria but not against type B. Type B was responsible for the college meningitis outbreaks in the United States in 2013 and causes about 90 percent of the meningococcal illnesses in several European countries. Scientists were unable to develop a type B vaccine for many years because there are many substrains of type B bacteria, and their polysaccharide capsules do not provoke an immune response. The lack of an immune response results from the fact that these capsules are biochemically similar to several types of human brain cells. The human immune system thus perceives these bacteria as "self" and does not produce antibodies against them.

Researchers therefore focused on making vaccines that contain bacterial surface proteins that do trigger an immune response. Scientists at Novartis Pharmaceuticals incorporated several such proteins into a new vaccine called Bexsero®. This vaccine was approved for use in several European countries and Australia in January 2013. Novartis is currently conducting Phase 3 clinical trials of this drug in the United States. Another

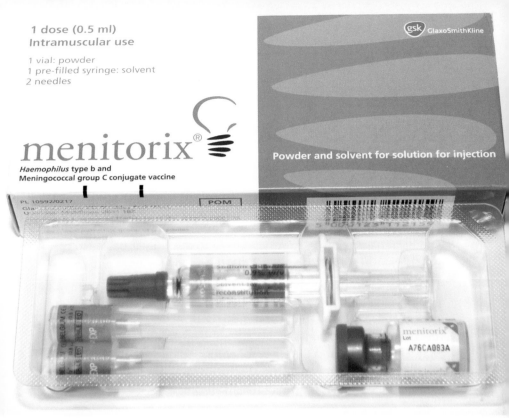

Menitorix is one of the many meningitis vaccines that have been developed in recent years.

drug company, Pfizer, is testing a similar type B vaccine known as rLP2086, which uses two types of bacterial surface proteins. This vaccine is intended specifically for adolescents.

Even though new type B vaccines are becoming available, a team of researchers headed by Christopher Bayliss of the University of Leicester in England cautions that the battle against these bacteria is not over: "It is not clear whether these vaccines will be able to prevent disease caused by all the different strains of MenB. There is, therefore, still a need to identify new targets on the bacteria, which can be developed as vaccine components to improve the effectiveness of these vaccines."[60] Bayliss's team is studying two bacterial proteins known as NalP and MspA that may be viable as vaccine targets.

Another shortcoming of the type B vaccines being tested is that they do not cause the human immune system to produce large quantities of antibodies. Researchers at the University of Oxford seek to overcome this shortcoming by attaching bacterial

Cultural Factors Affect Treatment

Sometimes cultural factors, along with medical limitations, affect disease treatment. For instance, many mothers of newborn infants with bacterial meningitis in Africa refuse to allow their babies to receive the fifty-eight injections (four injections per day for two weeks) of either penicillin or gentamicin needed to cure the disease. It is common for these mothers to take their babies home from hospitals before treatment is completed, both due to the cost of so many injections and because of the burden of remaining away from the rest of their family for so long. Many of these babies end up dying after they leave the hospital. In fact, about 50 percent of affected babies die from bacterial meningitis in Africa.

Researchers in Malawi are studying methods of improving survival in these infants. They are now testing the safety and effectiveness of using ceftriaxone in babies under two months old. This drug is currently approved for use in older children, requires only one injection per day, and is inexpensive enough to use in impoverished areas. The researchers believe that African mothers may be receptive to having their newborns treated with this drug if it proves to be safe and effective.

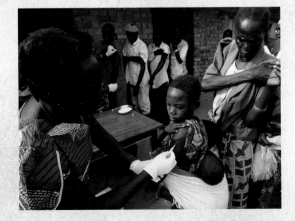

An African child receives a vaccination for meningitis. Fifty percent of African babies infected with bacterial meningitis die from it.

proteins to an inactivated virus that produces a robust immune response. These researchers are inserting bacterial proteins into inactivated adenoviruses. Active adenoviruses cause colds. The Oxford team writes, "The virus is very effective at triggering an immune response as the immune system is tricked into thinking it is fighting a real infection when it is actually facing a harmless vaccine."[61] The researchers are currently testing the vaccine on laboratory mice.

Meningitis in the Future

Effective meningococcal type B vaccines, along with existing vaccines, may bring medical science closer to controlling bacterial meningitis in the future. In 2012 Paul Offit of the Children's Hospital of Philadelphia stated, "By 2017 we should have—with the technologies currently underway—a viable and effective group B vaccine, and with a strategy of routine immunizations, we may be able to eliminate meningococci as a significant source of human disease."[62] However, other experts point out that the ability of meningococci to mutate into new strains may complicate efforts to eradicate these bacteria.

Other types of meningitis still pose a threat as well, so it is likely that the disease will continue to evoke widespread fear in the foreseeable future. Recent events illustrate that even isolated cases can lead to panic. For example, in May 2013 officials temporarily closed the Lindblom Math and Science Academy in Chicago after a student named Savon Smith died from bacterial meningitis. In July 2013 officials closed the water park where Kali Hardig contracted primary amoebic meningoencephalitis. In December 2013 Cristina Lete paid for her son Jacob to fly to London to receive a Bexsero® vaccination during the meningitis outbreak at the University of California–Santa Barbara. Emergency supplies of this vaccine were not authorized at this campus.

A 2013 article in the British scientific journal *Philosophical Transactions of the Royal Society* states that "throughout the nineteenth and twentieth centuries meningitis was one of the most feared infectious diseases, and it remains high in both public perception and as a public health priority."[63] At the same time, progress in treatment and prevention over the past century has drastically cut the number of meningitis infections and deaths. This fact, and ongoing research into further improvements, gives meningitis experts and the public hope that the effects of this disease will continue to diminish in the future.

Notes

Introduction: A Dreaded Disease

1. Quoted in MeningitisUK. "Patrons." http://212-110-189-141
.no-reverse-dns-set.bytemark.co.uk/about-us/meningitis-uk
-patrons.
2. Quoted in Abby Goodnough. "Sterility Found Lacking at
Drug Site in Outbreak." *New York Times*, October 23,
2012. www.nytimes.com/2012/10/24/health/sterility-found
-lacking-at-drug-site-in-meningitis-outbreak.html?_r=0.
3. Quoted in Senator Ed Markey. "Markey Applauds Passage
of Bipartisan Compounding Pharmacy Legislation." Press
release, November 18, 2013. www.markey.senate.gov
/record.cfm?id=348077.
4. Quoted in HealthDay. "As More Meningitis Cases Hit
Colleges, Experts Urge Awareness," November 26, 2013.
www.nlm.nih.gov/medlineplus/news/fullstory_142886
.html.
5. Quoted in Carla Rivera. "Students at UC Santa Barbara
Unsettled by Meningitis Outbreak." *Los Angeles Times*,
December 3, 2013. www.latimes.com/local/la-me-college
-outbreak- 20131204,0,2746711.story#axzz2pTGoiW5p.
6. Quoted in Rivera. "Students at UC Santa Barbara Unsettled by Meningitis Outbreak."
7. Andrew W. Artenstein. *In the Blink of an Eye*. New York:
Springer, 2013, p. 2.

Chapter One: What Is Meningitis?

8. Quoted in Martin W. Barr. *Cerebral Meningitis: Its History, Diagnosis, Prognosis, and Treatment*. Detroit: Da-
vis, 1892, p. 9.
9. Thomas Willis. *The London Practice of Physick: Or the
Whole Practical Part of Physick*. London: Basset, 1685.
http://books.google.com/books?id=iZ6Qnh_helkC&pg
=PA452.

10. Centers for Disease Control and Prevention. "Case File: Meningitis Mutants." www.cdc.gov/bam/diseases/immune /db/meningitis.html.

11. L. Danielson and E. Mann. "The History of a Singular and Very Mortal Disease Which Lately Made Its Appearance in Medfield." *Medical and Agricultural Register*, 1806, p. 65.

12. Quoted in Meningitis Research Foundation. "Jenny Dzafic." www.meningitis.org/book-of-experience/jenny -dzafic-26086.

13. National Foundation for Infectious Diseases. "Meningitis Myths and Facts for Consumers." www.nfid.org/idinfo /meningitis/consumers-myths.html.

14. Ask Dr. Sears. "Meningitis." www.askdrsears.com/topics /health-concerns/childhood-illnesses/meningitis.

Chapter Two: What Causes Meningitis?

15. Centers for Disease Control and Prevention. "Meningo-coccal Disease." wwwnc.cdc.gov/travel/yellowbook/2014 /chapter-3-infectious-diseases-related-to-travel/meningo coccal-disease.

16. Susan Lea. "Making the Paper." *Nature*, April 16, 2009, p. 805.

17. National Meningitis Association. "Is It Viral, Bacterial, or Fungal?" www.nmaus.org/disease-prevention-information /is-it-viral-bacterial-or-fungal.

18. Centers for Disease Control and Prevention. "Viral Menin-gitis." www.cdc.gov/meningitis/viral.html.

19. Robert H. Cowie. "Biology, Systematics, Life Cycle, and Distribution of *Angiostrongylus cantonensis*, the Cause of Rat Lungworm Disease." *Hawai'i Journal of Medicine & Public Health*, June 2013, p. 8.

20. Centers for Disease Control and Prevention. "Cryptococ-cal Infection." www.cdc.gov/fungal/pdf/at-a-glance-508c .pdf.

Chapter Three: Meningitis Treatment

21. Simon Flexner. "The Results of the Serum Treatment in Thirteen Hundred Cases of Epidemic Meningitis." *Journal*

of Experimental Medicine, May 1, 1913. http://jem.rupress
.org/content/17/5/553.full.pdf.

22. Artenstein, *In the Blink of an Eye,* p. 55.
23. Alexander Fleming. "Penicillin." Nobel Lecture, December 11, 1945. www.nobelprize.org/nobel_prizes/medicine
/laureates/1945/fleming-lecture.pdf.
24. Centers for Disease Control and Prevention. "Gram-Negative Bacteria Infections in Healthcare Settings." www.cdc.gov/hai/organisms/gram-negative-bacteria.html.
25. Diederik van de Beek et al. "Adjunctive Dexamethasone in Bacterial Meningitis: A Meta-analysis of Individual Patient Data." *Lancet Neurology,* March 2010, p. 254.
26. Quoted in National Meningitis Association. "Paisley." www.nmaus.org/story/paisley.
27. Quoted in National Meningitis Association. "Courtney." www.nmaus.org/story/courtney.
28. Sarah Jarvis. "Viral Meningitis—Never to Be Ignored." Patient.co.uk. www.patient.co.uk/blogs/sarah-says/2013
/05/viral-meningitis---never-to-be-ignored.
29. B. Mourvillier et al. "Induced Hypothermia in Severe Bacterial Meningitis: A Randomized Clinical Trial." *Journal of the American Medical Association,* November 27, 2013, p. 2174.

Chapter Four: Living with Meningitis

30. Quoted in Meningitis Foundation of America. "Sharon Cheslow." www.musa.org/cheslow.
31. Maree Selwood. "The Most Terrifying Day of My Life." Meningitis Centre of Australia. www.meningitis.com.au
/personal_stories/maree_selwood_shares_her_story.phtml.
32. Selwood. "The Most Terrifying Day of My Life."
33. Jane Danzi. "Cameron's Story." Meningitis Centre of Australia. www.meningitis.com.au/personal_stories/my
_story_cameron.phtml.
34. Quoted in Meningitis Centre of Australia. "Mikayla's Meningococcal Story." www.meningitis.com.au/personal
_stories/mikayla_s_meningococcal_story.phtml.
35. Bob Werner and Dee Dee Werner. "Bob & Dee Dee's Story." Confederation of Meningitis Organisations.

www.comomeningitis.org/personal-meningitis-stories
/bob-and-dee-dees-story.

36. Jimmy and Véronique. "Jimmy and Véronique's Story."
Confederation of Meningitis Organisations. www.como
meningitis.org/personal-meningitis-stories/jimmy-and
-véroniques-story.

37. Sammy-Jo Farrell. "Tess's Story." Meningitis NOW. www
.meningitisnow.org/how-we-help/our-support-services
/story-centre/tess-s-story.

38. Werner and Werner. "Bob and Dee Dee's Story."

39. Danzi. "Cameron's Story."

40. Quoted in Meningitis Foundation of America. "Keith
McIntyre." www.musa.org/mcintyre.

41. Quoted in Charlotte Dovey. "The Headaches That Feel
like Flu but Can Leave You Blind: Woman, 45, Is Horri-
fied to Discover She Actually Had Meningitis." *Daily Mail*
(London), August 20, 2013. www.dailymail.co.uk/health
/article-2397786/Dianne-Woodford-45-horrified-discover
-headaches-felt-like-flu-bacterial-MENINGITIS--left-blind
.html.

42. Andy Marso, *Worth the Pain: How Meningitis Nearly
Killed Me—Then Changed My Life for the Better*. Kansas
City: Kansas City Star Books, 2013, p. 13.

43. Quoted in National Meningitis Association. "Blake." www
.nmaus.org/story/blake.

44. Quoted in National Meningitis Association. "Ashley."
www.nmaus.org/story/ashley.

Chapter Five: Preventing Meningitis

45. Sumaiya Khan. "Bacterial Meningitis Precautions." *Buzzle*
(blog), February 4, 2010. www.buzzle.com/articles
/bacterial-meningitis-precautions.html.

46. Stefan Riedel. "Edward Jenner and the History of Smallpox and Vaccination." *Baylor University Medical Center
Proceedings*, January 2005. www.ncbi.nlm.nih.gov/pmc
/articles/PMC1200696.

47. Artenstein. *In the Blink of an Eye*, p. 84.

48. Centers for Disease Control and Prevention. "Prevention
and Control of Meningococcal Disease." *Morbidity and
Mortality Weekly Report*, March 22, 2013, p. 12.

49. David Stephens. "Protecting the Herd: The Remarkable Effectiveness of the Bacterial Meningitis Polysaccharide-Protein Conjugate Vaccines in Altering Transmission Dynamics." *Transactions of the American Clinical and Climatological Association*, vol. 22, 2011, p. 115.
50. Centers for Disease Control and Prevention. "Parasitic Meningitis." www.cdc.gov/meningitis/parasitic.html.

Chapter Six: The Future

51. Meningitis Research Foundation. "Impact of Meningitis Findings and Recommendations from the Member Survey." www.meningitis.org/impact-of-meningitis.
52. Quoted in University of Missouri School of Medicine News. "New Look at Old Test May Provide Earlier Detection of Meningitis, MU Researchers Find," October 2013. http://medicine.missouri.edu/news/0207.php.
53. Xijing Hospital. "Diagnosis of Tuberculous Meningitis by ESAT-6 in CSF." Clinical Trials.gov, January 31, 2013. http://clinicaltrials.gov/ct2/show/NCT01371916?recr=open &cond=%22Meningitis%22&rank=5.
54. University Hospital Inselspital. "Daptomycin in Pediatric Patients with Bacterial Meningitis." Clinical Trials.gov, March 3, 2014. http://clinicaltrials.gov/ct2/show/study/NC T01522105?recr=Open&cond=%22Meningitis%22&rank=6 &show_desc=Y#desc.
55. Quoted in Meningitis Research Foundation. "Adult Meningitis Caused by Herpes Viruses." www.meningitis.org /current-projects/adult-meningitis-caused-by-029901.
56. Bing Zhai et al. "The Antidepressant Sertraline Provides a Promising Therapeutic Option for Neurotropic Cryptococcal Infections." *Antimicrobial Agents and Chemotherapy*, July 2012. www.ncbi.nlm.nih.gov/pmc/articles /PMC3393448.
57. Centers for Disease Control and Prevention. "CDC Issues Update on Multistate Outbreak of Fungal Meningitis and Other Infections: One Year Later." Infection Control Today. www.infectioncontroltoday.com/news/2013/10 /cdc-issues-update-on-multistate-outbreak-of-fungal -meningitis-and-other-infections-one-year-later.aspx.

58. C.M.C. Rodrigues et al. "Complement Factor H Genotype and Protein Levels Associated with the Clinical Sepsis Phenotype in Children with Meningococcal Disease." Meningitis Research Foundation. www.meningitis.org /posters.

59. Jean-Marc Collard et al. "Epidemiological Changes in Meningococcal Meningitis in Niger from 2008 to 2011 and the Impact of Vaccination." *BMC Infectious Diseases*, December 6, 2013, p. 576.

60. Quoted in Meningitis Research Foundation. "Examination of Two Meningococcal Surface Proteins as Potential Vaccine Targets." www.meningitis.org/current-projects /examination-of-two-38025.

61. Quoted in Meningitis NOW. "Using a Virus to Create a New Meningitis B Vaccine." www.meningitisnow.org/how -we-help/research/our-research-projects/using-a-virus-to -create-a-new-meningitis-b-vaccine.

62. Quoted in Artenstein. *In the Blink of an Eye*, p. 105.

63. Martin C.J. Maiden. "The Impact of Protein-Conjugate Polysaccharide Vaccines: An Endgame for Meningitis?" *Philosophical Transactions of the Royal Society*, June 24, 2013. http://rstb.royalsocietypublishing.org/content /368/1623/20120147.full.pdf.

Glossary

antibiotic: A drug that kills bacteria.

antibody: A chemical produced by the immune system to neutralize a specific antigen.

antigen: A foreign protein or organism that stimulates an immune attack.

arachnoid mater: The middle layer of the meninges.

aseptic meningitis: Meningitis caused by factors other than bacteria.

blood-brain barrier: A network of tightly packed cells that protect the central nervous system.

central nervous system: The brain and spinal cord.

cerebrospinal fluid: The liquid that surrounds the brain and spinal cord.

contagious: A type of disease that has the ability to spread from person to person.

dura mater: The outer layer of the meninges.

epidemic: Many cases of a particular disease.

immune system: The cells and chemicals that defend the body against attack.

infectious: A type of disease that is spread by microorganisms.

meninges: The membranes that line the brain and spinal cord.

meningitis: An inflammation of the meninges.

meningococcemia: Blood poisoning resulting from infection with meningococcal bacteria.

microorganism: A tiny organism that can only be seen with a microscope.

neuron: A nerve cell.

pathogen: A disease-causing organism.

peripheral nervous system: The nerve network outside the central nervous system.

pia mater: The innermost layer of the meninges.

sepsis: Blood poisoning.

serogroup: A group of cells or microorganisms that contain common surface antigens.

spinal tap: A procedure in which doctors remove cerebrospinal fluid from the spine.

vaccine: A drug that prevents people or animals from getting sick from a particular pathogen.

Organizations to Contact

Centers for Disease Control and Prevention (CDC)

1600 Clifton Rd.
Atlanta, GA 30333
(800) 232-4636
www.cdc.gov

The CDC is a government agency that formulates public health policies, provides disease statistics, and offers information on all aspects of meningitis.

Confederation of Meningitis Organisations (CoMO)

PO Box 855, West Perth
Western Australia 6872
+61 8 389 7308
www.comomeningitis.org

CoMO is an international organization that brings patient groups, health professionals, and meningitis organizations from around the world together to raise awareness of the disease and to advocate for government-sponsored prevention programs.

Meningitis Foundation of America

PO Box 1818
El Mirage, AZ 85335
(480) 270-2652
www.musa.org

The Meningitis Foundation of America is a nonprofit organization that supports people affected by meningitis, educates the public, and promotes meningitis research and prevention.

National Foundation for Infectious Diseases (NFID)

7201 Wisconsin Ave., Ste. 750

Bethesda, MD 20814

(301) 656-0003

www.nfid.org

The NFID is a nonprofit organization that educates the public about all aspects of infectious diseases.

National Institute of Allergy and Infectious Diseases (NIAID)

National Institutes of Health

6610 Rockledge Dr., MSC 6612

Bethesda, MD 20892

(301) 496-5717

www.niaid.nih.gov

The NIAID is a branch of the National Institutes of Health that sponsors and conducts research on the infectious aspects of meningitis. It also offers public information on all aspects of the disease.

National Institute of Neurological Disorders and Stroke (NINDS)

PO Box 5801

Bethesda, MD 20824

(800) 352-9424

www.ninds.nih.gov

The NINDS is a government agency and a branch of the National Institutes of Health that sponsors and conducts research on brain disorders, including meningitis, and offers general information about the nervous system and meningitis.

National Meningitis Association

PO Box 725165
Atlanta, GA 31139
(866) 366-3662
www.nmaus.org

The nonprofit National Meningitis Association supports and educates people affected by meningitis, educates the public, and raises funds for meningitis research.

World Health Organization (WHO)

Avenue Appia 20
1211 Geneva 27
Switzerland
+41 22 791 21 11
www.who.int

The WHO is the United Nations' health authority. It provides information and sets standards for global health concerns such as meningitis.

For More Information

Books

Connie Goldsmith. *Meningitis*. Minneapolis: Twenty-First Century, 2007. This book for teens discusses all aspects of meningitis.

Hal Marcovitz. *Meningitis*. San Diego: ReferencePoint, 2008. Written for teens, this book presents summaries of information about symptoms, prevention, treatment, and social impacts of meningitis, to be used by students writing reports on the subject.

Andy Marso, *Worth the Pain*. Kansas City, MO: Kansas City Star Books, 2013. A young man's personal experience journey after meningitis.

Brian R. Shmaefsky. *Meningitis*. New York: Chelsea House, 2010. This book for teens focuses on diagnosis, causes, prevention, treatment, and research.

Internet Sources

Center for Young Women's Health, Boston Children's Hospital. "Meningococcal Vaccine." www.youngwomenshealth.org /mening.html.

Centers for Disease Control and Prevention. "Case File: Meningitis Mutants." www.cdc.gov/bam/diseases/immune/db /meningitis.html.

Websites

"Killer Disease on Campus," *NOVA* (www.pbs.org/wgbh/nova /meningitis). Features interviews, articles, and videos about meningitis on college campuses.

Meningitis, MedlinePlus (www.nlm.nih.gov/medlineplus /tutorials/meningitis/htm/index.htm). An interactive tutorial program about all aspects of meningitis.

Meningitis, TeensHealth (http://kidshealth.org/teen/infections /bacterial_viral/meningitis.html#cat20174). This teen website describes all aspects of meningitis.

Neuroscience for Kids (https://faculty.washington.edu/chu dler/neurok.html). This website explores the nervous system with fun experiments and facts.

Index

A
Acyclovir, 51, 83
Africa
  cryptococcal meningitis in, 36
  cultural factors and treatment in, 90
  meningitis belt in, 29
  vaccination efforts in, 87–88
Amoebic meningoencephalitis, primary, 34, 83, 91
Amphotericin B, 51, 83
Angiostrongyliasis (eosinophilic meningitis), 34
Angiostrongylus cantonensis (rat lungworm), 33–34
Antibiotics, 43–44
Antibodies, 40
Antibody titer, 72
Antifungal drugs, 51
Antiserum therapy, 40–43
Arachnoid mater, 14
Artenstein, Malcolm, 69

B
Bacteria, 35
  drug resistance in, 44, 46
Baylor University Medical Center Proceedings (journal), 68
Becky Werner Meningitis Foundation, 58, 60
Behcet's disease, 38

Blood-brain barrier, 14–15
  meningococcal breach of, 26
Blood tests, 23
Bozof, Lynn, 76, 77
Brain
  damage from pneumococcal meningitis, research on preventing, 82–83
  permanent damage of, from bacterial meningitis, 58–59
Brudzinski, Josef, 17
Brudzinski's sign, 16, 17

C
Carcinomatosis meningitis, 39
  treatment of, 52–53
CDC (Centers for Disease Control and Prevention), 7, 30, 31
Cefotaxime, 46
Centers for Disease Control and Prevention (CDC), 7, 30, 31
Central nervous system (CNS), 13–14
Cephalosporin, 46, 47
Cerebral cortex, 59
Cerebrospinal fluid, 14
  analysis of, 23
Choroid plexus, 14
Coal tar, 43
Coccidioides immitis (fungus), 37–38

Coccidioides posadasii
(fungus), 37–38
Commission on Meningitis, 69
Complement factor H gene,
86–87
Computed tomography (CT)
scan, 23
Corticosteroids, 48
Cryptococcal meningitis,
35–37
research into treatment of,
83–84, 87
Cryptococcus neoformans
(fungus), 35–37, *37*
Cytokines, 38, 62

D
Danielson, Lothario, 13
Daptomycin, 82
Death rate(s), 6
Dexamethasone, 48, 81
Diagnosis, 20–23
research into, 79–80
Dihydropteroate synthase,
44
Drug-induced meningitis, 38
Drug Quality and Security Act
(2013), 9
Dura mater, 13–14

E
Endotoxin, 26
Eosinophilic meningitis
(angiostrongyliasis), 34
Exserohilum rostratum, 7

F
Falx cerebri, 14
FDA. *See* Food and Drug
Administration, U.S.

Fleming, Alexander, 44, 45, *45*
Flexner, Simon, 40–43, *41*
Folic acid, 44
Food and Drug
Administration, U.S. (FDA),
9, 71, 76, 85
Fungal meningitis, 34–38
prevention of, 75–76
research on treatment of,
84
treatment of, 51
Fungi, 35

G
Guillain-Barré syndrome
(GBS), 72

H
Haemophilus influenzae type
B (Hib), 30, *31*
vaccine for, 70–71
Herd immunity, 72–74
Herpin, François, 11
Hippocampus, 59

I
Imaging studies, 23

J
Jenner, Edward, *67*, 67–68
*Journal of the American
Medical Association*, 52

K
Kernig's sign, 16–17
Kitasato, Shibasaburo, 42

L
Lancet Neurology (journal),
48

LCMV (lymphocytic
  choriomeningitis virus),
  32–33, 75
Listeria monocytogenes, 30
  prevention of infection by,
  75
Lumbar puncture (spinal tap),
  22, *22*
Lymphocytic
  choriomeningitis virus
  (LCMV), 32–33
  prevention of, 75

M
Magnetic resonance imaging
  (MRI), 23
Mann, Elias, 13
Markey, Edward, 9
Marso, Andy, 63, *64*
Meninges, 11, *15*
  inflammation of, 14–17
  role of, 13–14
Meningitis
  bacterial, 29–30
  carcinomatosis, 39, 52–53
  cryptococcal, 35–37
  definition of, 11
  drug-induced, 38
  1806 Massachusetts
    outbreak, 15
  long-term effects of, 55–56,
    58–61
  meningococcal, 9–10, 24–26,
    26–29
  parasitic, 33–34, 77–78
  protozoa causing, *16*
  rates of, by age group/
    burden of disease, *8*
  screening for, 49–50
  smoking and, 28

symptoms of, 15–17
  type B, 9–10
  viral, 30–33
  See also Symptoms;
    Treatment(s); *specific
    types*
Meningitis Research
  Foundation, 79
Meningitis Vaccine Project,
  87
Meningococcal meningitis
  risk factors for, 26–27, 29
  smoking and, 28
  transmission of, 26
  type B, 9–10, 88–89, 90
Meningococcemia
  (meningococcal sepsis), 18
Meningococci, 24–25, *86*
  subtypes of, 25–26
Menitorix, *89*
Miltefosine, 52, 83
Mollaret, Pierre, 32
Mollaret meningitis, 31–32

N
Naegleria fowleri (amoeba),
  34, 51–52
  prevention of infection by,
  77–78
National Foundation for
  Infectious Diseases, 20
National Meningitis
  Association, 29, 76
NECC (New England
  Compounding Center), 7, *7*,
  8–9
Neisseria meningitidis, 25
  vaccine for, 68
New England Compounding
  Center (NECC), 7, *7*, 8–9

O
Ommaya reservoir, 46

P
Parasites, 35
Parasitic meningitis, 33–34
  prevention of, 77–78
  research on treatment of, 84
Pasteur, Louis, *25*
Penicillin, 44, 45
Peptidoglycan, 44
Phenytoin, 82–83
Pia mater, 14
Pneumococcus
  (*Streptococcus
  pneumoniae*), 29
Polymerase chain reaction, 23
Princeton University, 2013
  meningococcal outbreak at,
  9–10

R
Rat lungworms, 33–34
Research
  on causes of meningitis,
  84–87
  on improved diagnosis,
  79–81
  on prevention, 87–88
  on treatment of bacterial
  meningitis, 81–83
  on treatment of nonbacterial
  meningitis, 83–84
  on type B meningococcal
  vaccines, 88–89, 91

S
Sarcoidosis, 38
Selwood, Adam, 56, *56*
Sepsis, 18, 86

Sertraline (Zoloft), 84
Smallpox, 66–67
Smoking, meningococcal
  disease and, 28
Streptococcus pneumoniae
  (pneumococcus), 29
Subarachnoid space, 14
Sulfonamides (sulfa drugs),
  43–44
Symptoms, 15–17, *21*
  variation in, 17–20

T
Transmission, of
  meningococcal meningitis,
  26
Treatment(s)
  antiserum therapy, 40–43
  for bacterial meningitis,
  research on, 81–83
  cultural factors in, 90
  of fungal meningitis, 51
  for noninfectious
  meningitis, 52–53
  prompt, importance of,
  48–50
  for viral meningitis,
  research on, 83
Tuberculous meningitis
  (TBM), 80

U
Ulcerative colitis, 30

V
Vaccines/vaccinations, 6, 9,
  73
  booster, 72
  conjugate, 70
  early, 66–68

efforts to increase
  awareness of, 76–77
for *Haemophilus
  influenzae* type B, 30
improvements in, 68–69
opposition to, 74
for pneumococcal
  meningitis, 71
quadrivalent, 69
side effects of, 71–72
for type B meningococcal
  meningitis, 88–89, 91

Valley fever, 37–38
Variolation, 66–67
Viral meningitis, 30–33
  rash caused by, *32*
Viruses, 35
Von Behring, Emil, 42

W
Weichselbaum, Anton, 24
Willis, Thomas, 11, 12, *12*
World Health Organization, 87
Worth the Pain (Marso), 63

Picture Credits

About the Author

Melissa Abramovitz has been a writer for more than twenty-five years and specializes in writing nonfiction magazine articles and books for all age groups. She is the author of hundreds of magazine articles, more than thirty educational books for children and teenagers, numerous poems and short stories, and several children's picture books. Her book for writers, *A Treasure Trove of Opportunity: How to Write and Sell Articles for Children's Magazines*, has been widely acclaimed since its publication in 2012. She is a graduate of the University of California–San Diego and the Institute of Children's Literature and is a member of the Society of Children's Book Writers and Illustrators and the Working Writer's Club. Visit her website at www.melissaabramovitz.com.